Atlantic Adventure

by Francis Chichester

ALONE ACROSS THE ATLANTIC
ASTRO-NAVIGATION
OBSERVER'S PLANISPHERE OF AIRNAVIGATION STARS

Francis Chichester

ATLANTIC
ADVENTURE

EDITED BY

J. R. L. ANDERSON
Yachting Editor of 'The Guardian'

London
GEORGE ALLEN & UNWIN LTD
RUSKIN HOUSE   MUSEUM STREET

PRINTED IN GREAT BRITAIN
in 10 point Plantin type
BY C. TINLING AND CO. LTD.,
LIVERPOOL, LONDON AND PRESCOT

CONTENTS

Introduction

BY J.R.L. ANDERSON

JANUARY 1962 came in with one of the vilest stretches of weather that even the English climate can produce. 'They order things better at sea,' I thought, as I made my way to the Boat Show through the chaos that afflicts road, rail, and bus transport in England every time there is a fall of snow. A full gale off Cape Horn would have been taken by the crew of a sailing vessel in a more matter of fact way than London takes a few inches of snow. The weather is relevant to this story: those detestable days in early January were certainly one of the reasons why the first discussion of Francis Chichester's project at his house on the evening of January 6th fired the imagination. And the weather dogged us afterwards: a wretchedly cold spring and early summer interfered seriously with the tasks of fitting-out, and sent plans for numerous trial trips in *Gipsy Moth III* spinning. The splendid achievement of Francis's record-breaking voyage in 1962 was carried out against a background of delays and frustrations, mainly brought about by the weather.

But much of this is private history; of no consequence against the later reality of Francis's achievement. What happened was this: at that time I was Vice-Commodore of the Silhouette Owners' Association, a body uniting those of us who sail in that remarkable small sailing cruiser known as the Silhouette. I had corresponded with Francis on one or two matters in the past, and I asked him if he would present the trophies, won for various events during the year, at an annual party that the Association holds in London. Generously, he said that he would, and he invited me to go along to his house first for a drink. It was while we were sitting chatting in the beautiful drawing-room of his house in St James's Place that he rather casually mentioned that he was thinking of making a single-handed crossing of the Atlantic again. He had won the world's first single-handed Transatlantic race in 1960 in a time of forty and a half days from Plymouth to New York, surviving a great gale, and beating his nearest rival, Colonel J. G. Hasler, in *Jester*, by a clear eight days. He had been presented with a trophy by the Duke of Edinburgh, and he had been acclaimed 'Yachtsman of the Year'.

That, one might think, would be enough for any man, particularly a man approaching sixty-one. Not so for Francis. He had been disappointed with his own performance in 1960, and he thought that he ought to be able to do better. He had lost four days during a gale, and he thought that there ought to be at least a statistical chance of making a passage without meeting a severe Atlantic gale. (There may be a statistical chance of this, but it didn't turn up on the 1962 voyage.) Anyway, he wanted to have another go.

But a single-handed passage in a small sailing boat is about the most expensive way of crossing the Atlantic known to man. True, one can be penniless and lucky in some old boat held together by hope, and potter down through the trade winds to the West Indies, do some island hopping, and hope ultimately to make New York. But that was not what Francis wanted: he did not want to potter, he wanted to race. And he did not want the easy run of a trade wind passage: he wanted to drive himself and his boat more or less across across the Great Circle route direct from Plymouth to New York, knowing that on an east-west crossing he would have the currents of the Gulf Stream against him all the time, and a chance of headwinds for much of the time. This sort of passage cannot be attempted in an old boat held together by hope.

Francis had a fine ship in *Gipsy Moth III*, designed by Robert Clark, and built by John Tyrrell at Arklow in 1959. But *Gipsy Moth* is big for single-handed sailing: she is all but 40 feet long, 13 tons Thames Measurement, and her gear is a formidable weight for one man to tackle. Against this, she existed, she belonged to Francis, and she was unquestionably strong enough for the job. But Francis had not been altogether pleased with her performance under her original sloop rig—that is, with a large mainsail, and a single foresail or jib. He had called in John Illingworth, one of the greatest ocean racers of all time, and among the best of modern yacht designers. Illingworth suggested that *Gipsy* should be re-rigged as a cutter, to divide her headsail area among two sails, a jib and staysail, and to reduce the area of her mainsail a little. Cutter rig, although theoretically not quite so efficient aerodynamically as the Bermudan sloop rig, would have other advantages for single-handed sailing and, Illingworth thought, would make *Gipsy Moth* somewhat better balanced.

Francis also wanted to replace his original wooden mast with a spar of metal alloy. All this would be expensive, and then there would be all the other costs of the expedition. Would the *Guardian*, Francis asked, consider contributing to the costs in return for the narrative of the voyage?

This was not easy to answer. I told Francis that personally I was greatly interested, of course, and would do whatever I could to help, but that the decision on the financial side of things could be made only by the Editor, Alastair Hetherington. We discussed things a bit more, and the idea that finally made his crossing one of the most remarkable newspaper achievements for many years was born. Francis said that Marconi Marine had offered to equip *Gipsy* with a small battery-operated radiotelephone, with a theoretical range of perhaps 3,000–4,000 miles. If this worked, could we, as a newspaper, carry a daily account of his voyage while he was actually making it? It was an exciting idea. There have been many small boat voyages, and many fine books written about them, but these had all been written, or at least published, after the voyage was made. For a single-handed navigator, alone in the North Atlantic ocean, to be in touch with the world by telephone was something quite new. The question was, could it be done?

The odds seemed, on the whole, against it. Radio at the best of times is inclined to be eccentric, and a radiotelephone in a small boat seemed to have pretty well everything against it. On a big ship radio aerials can be insulated efficiently, but on a small sailing boat this presented many difficulties. Moreover, salt water is a constant enemy to everything electrical, and large areas of spray-drenched sail are about the worst thing possible to have in the vicinity of a radiotelephone. However, these were all fairly obvious difficulties, and there might be ways of overcoming them. I went to see Mr G. F. Wilson, Assistant Inspector of Wireless

Telegraphy in the Marine Radio Department of the Post Office, to ask his views on the project. Mr Wilson already knew of the proposal, because Francis had discussed the idea with Captain F. J. Wylie and Mr Eric Stride, of the Radio Advisory Service, and they had interested the Post Office in it. The help of the Radio Advisory Service was invaluable.

Mr Wilson called in Mr S. W. Woolford of the External Telecommunications Executive, who would be deeply involved if the venture actually came off, and we had a long talk about things. Expert opinion was that if the radio-telephone could be satisfactorily installed—a fairly big 'if'—it could be expected to work, but that it was unlikely to give much in the way of reception beyond 40 degrees west of Greenwich. New York is 73 degrees 50 minutes west of Greenwich, so that 40 degrees west was little more than halfway. But there was more to it than this. Expert opinion is bound to be cautious, but the best experts are always ready to experiment.

The Post Office would guarantee nothing in the way of radio reception—indeed it could not—but Mr Wilson offered all the facilities of his department, and we all wanted to have a go. The chances were against good reception beyond 40 degrees west, but the radio might go on working well beyond that point. Nobody could say what would really happen, because such an experiment had never before been tried.

I reported all this back to Alastair Hetherington in Manchester, and Francis and Sheila Chichester came down to see him. We had another long discussion, and the upshot was that the *Guardian* agreed to come in on the adventure. It was a gamble, we might very well lose contact with Francis and *Gipsy Moth* after the first few days, but if the radio worked it would be a wonderful achievement, so we went ahead.

All this was at the end of January and early February. Francis and Sheila went off to France for a brief holiday, and it was arranged that fitting-out should begin seriously in March. *Gipsy* was lying at the Agamemnon Yard at Buckler's Hard on the Beaulieu River, and on March 8th I drove down there to meet Francis. It was a bitterly cold day. It was too early in the season for the hotel at Buckler's Hard to be open, but a small bar was, and we lunched on beer and some biscuits and cheese that I had brought down with me.

In spite of the weather, we were a cheerful party—Francis and Sheila, Mr D. J. Darby, and Mr D. R. Watson, two Marconi Marine technologists, and later John Illingworth. *Gipsy* was in a shed at Buckler's Hard, stripped, with her mast unstepped, and looking as miserable as boats out of their element always do. She was unwrapped by the yard people, and we went on board for hours of discussion and measuring about all that had to be done. It seemed endless.

However, plans were made, and everybody got down to work. *Gipsy*'s new metal mast had been made and had arrived, and the special steel wire rope for her rigging, made by John Shaw at Worksop, was well in hand. The rigging had to have specially designed terminals, which were being made by M. S. Gibb at Warsash, and we went to see Mr Gibb, who promised to do everything he could to get them made promptly. The original intention was that *Gipsy*'s mast should be stepped at the end of March, leaving the whole of April and May for sailing trials. This did not happen, because the appalling weather held up everything, and it was not until nearly the end of April that Francis was able to take her out for her first sailing trials under her new rig. He describes these himself in his own narrative later.

On May 11th I joined him at Portsmouth to accompany him on extended trials in the Channel. The Navy had generously lent *Gipsy* a mooring off Whale Island, and we intended to sail with the Royal Ocean Racing Club's fleet on the Lyme Bay race from Southsea. We didn't expect to do much in the way of racing against fully-manned ocean racing yachts, but Francis wanted to see how *Gipsy*, sailed single-handed, would keep up. I was simply a passenger: I had agreed that Francis should do everything single-handed, and my sole function was to keep watch in the busy shipping lanes of the Channel while Francis got some rest. This trip was interesting rather than anything else. It started badly. We were lying off Whale Island, surrounded by the somewhat muted might of England in the form of a number of cocooned warships. When the time came to leave our mooring there was scarcely any wind at all to take us to Southsea, and Francis decided to motor down there under *Gipsy*'s engine. He went to start the engine, and then he looked up through the hatch. 'Do you think' he said, 'that an engine will go without any oil at all?' I said that this seemed extremely improbable. Francis had sailed over from Buckler's Hard, and by some miserable mischance the oil filler cap had been left off, thus every time *Gipsy* heeled, oil had run out from the engine. There was a fearful mess in the tray under the engine, and no oil showing on the dipstick at all.

'Well,' said Francis, 'we are supposed to be a sailing ship, so we shall have to try to get ourselves out under sail.' There seemed a breath of wind, so he hoisted the mainsail and we cast off our mooring. But the breath of wind was rippling the water a couple of hundred yards away: where we were, we were completely blanketed by the cocooned warships. We began drifting slowly towards one of them.

'There might be a scrap of oil in the sump,' Francis said, 'and the only thing to do is to see if we can run the engine long enough to get out into the fairway.' He pressed the starter, the engine fired, and we began to move. I was at the tiller, and there seemed plenty of water to get clear. The next moment we were aground. What was worse, it was about ten minutes off high water.

It looked as if our Channel trials would be spent hard on the mud off Whale Island. Francis got out a kedge, and we hauled as hard as we could, but *Gipsy* would not budge. A small naval motor boat came up and took a line, but still she would not budge. Salvation suddenly appeared in the shape of Captain Peter Thompson, R.M., with a large and powerful marine picket boat. She took a line and *Gipsy* slid thankfully off the bank. The engine ran long enough to get us into the fairway, and we were clear.

We ran slowly down to Southsea to make the starting line for the RORC race, and just about managed it, but it was miserable sailing. There was next to no wind, it was bitterly cold, and a succession of thunderstorms flung buckets of freezing rain at us. The RORC fleet set spinakers, and began to disappear over the horizon. We decided to experiment with the radiotelephone. It was not a very successful experiment. We had to call Niton Radio in the Isle of Wight, and local thunderstorms made conditions difficult. However, we got through in the end, and established contact with David Fairhall, the *Guardian*'s Shipping Correspondent, who was waiting to receive the call at the Post Office's Marine Radio Terminal at Brent. The best that could be said was that we got through. Then we settled down to sail. We had pretty well everything during the night from dead calm to a Force 8 wind. There was a bad moment when Francis hurt his hand when a spar to boom out the jib jumped from the socket to which he was fitting it, but what might have been a horrid accident mercifully turned out to be no more than a bad scrape. Francis tried *Gipsy* under various combinations of sail, and she behaved well. Next morning we tried the radiotelephone again. We got through much better, and Francis was able to report that *Gipsy* was hard on the wind, doing a good 7 knots.

We made our way back to the Isle of Wight and Portsmouth, and the final beat up the Channel from Southsea was fun. There was a decent wind, and Francis sailed *Gipsy* like a dinghy, racing close in to the promenade at Southsea before going about. She turned on her heel like a dinghy, and behaved magnificently. It was a splendid sail.

Francis was due to leave Plymouth for his crossing to New York on June 1st, so there was little more than three weeks left for all that had to be done. How everything got done I still don't know, but it did get done. The Marconi people did a wonderful job of installation on the radio. The 'Kestrel' transmitter/receiver was installed in a space about as big as that taken up by a table-top domestic refrigerator, just inside the cabin hatch. A twenty-four-volt bank of 'Exide' batteries was placed in a specially lined acid proof tray. Near them was the small petrol-driven generator for charging them. Mr W. Maconachie, of Marconi Marine, wrote an article about the installation for the *Guardian*, and I cannot do better than quote from it. 'The installation of the transmitter and batteries,' he wrote, 'was fairly routine stuff, and not much more difficult than a similar exercise on one of the smaller fishing craft that use radio equipment of this type. On the aerial/earth side things were different. Earthing on this wooden boat was arranged through a copper plate fixed to the outside of the hull, well below waterline level to allow for lying over, with an earth bolt brought inboard through the planking. The greatest length of aerial run on a line least likely to be obstructed by sail movement was found from close to the masthead to the port and starboard rails abaft the break of the cabin positions already occupied by backstays. The thing to do was to replace the backstays by aerials, while retaining the strength of the stays so that the aerials could do a double job. This was accomplished by providing special stays of stranded stainless steel, broken just below masthead and above deck by twin insulators of a high breaking strain, and splicing into the lower end of each stainless steel aerial a connecting "tail" ending in a spring battery clip of the crocodile type. This arrangement provides two independent transmitting aerials, close together at the top, and separated by the beam of the boat at deck level.' The twin aerials were necessary to provide a working aerial unobstructed by the mainsail on whichever tack Gipsy might be lying over. Separate receiving aerials, independent of the transmitting aerials, were also fitted. The best position for these was judged to be that already occupied by the shrouds, but the pattern for the transmitting aerials on the backstays could not be followed, because even high strain insulators might have introduced a dangerous weakness into the vital shrouds. Instead, a length of insulated wire was taped tightly to the inboard side of the shrouds, and the ends taken down through the deck to the receiver.

Victualling and stores for the voyage were looked after by Sheila Chichester, and the job was described by David Fairhall in an article we published shortly before the start of the trip. He wrote: 'Scurvy may be something of a medical curiosity these days, but providing a constant supply of fresh food is still the basic problem when victualling a yacht for an ocean voyage. This, at any rate, is Mrs Francis Chichester's main preoccupation as she prepares for her husband's transatlantic crossing in June. With a large crew water supplies would also be difficult, but Mr Chichester will be alone when he sets out from Plymouth to beat his own record of forty days for the westward crossing.

'Right at the top of the stores list, therefore, come two dozen lemons, supported by oranges and apples, sixteen tins of fruit, and three dozen bottles of juices and cordial. There will also be a good deal of dried fruit on board, including dried bananas, which proved successful on previous trips.

'The Chichesters are basically vegetarian, so that having satisfied the need for Vitamin C the rest of the food stores are centred on cheeses, eggs, and nuts. The cheeses can presumably look after themselves for a few weeks, but even new laid eggs would not survive the crossing under normal conditions. About half of the nine dozen will therefore be coated with "Oateg" preservative by Mrs Martin, who is supplying most of the general stores down at Buckler's Hard. The potatoes will be packed in small plastic bags, containing perhaps a day's supply and provided with air holes to prevent them sweating.

'These methods were tried out successfully during the single-handed transatlantic race in 1960 and Mrs Chichester seems to have made few changes in her victualling plans this time. Perhaps her fundamental principle is to keep every aspect of the affair, from buying to the final stowage, under her own supervision. Least of all would she leave it to her husband, who is likely to be far too preoccupied with handling *Gipsy Moth III* to remember what he needs to be on board—or where he has stowed it.

'On a trip like this, where every fraction of a knot counts every hour of the day, food and sleep are necessary evils rather than luxuries to be enjoyed. The aim is therefore to keep stores as near as possible to where they are required, in the most convenient form. There will be no anonymous tins swilling around in the bilges, which turn out to contain apricots instead of tomato soup when you open them. One of the few things down there will be methylated spirit, arranged in bottles just by the Primus stove. Unless you have been to sea in a small boat like this one, it is difficult to conceive how much you can appreciate something being at your feet instead of on the other side of the cabin.

'A more serious matter is the design of the petrol cans, which are painted a different colour from those containing paraffin. Petrol spilt into the bilges could be disastrous, so small cans fitted with suitable spouts and handles have been provided to be filled from larger ones. Obvious labour savers like "Thermos" flasks and tea bags will naturally be used and all the nuts will be shelled beforehand.

'In the detailed planning of her husband's diet, Mrs Chichester has tried to combine simplicity with variety.

'Many of his meals will be based on fried potatoes and onions, but Chinook salmon, soft roes, anchovies, smoked salmon and similar delicacies should counteract any tendency to culinary boredom. A typical menu might be:

Breakfast: Grapefruit segments or Muesli (made with Frutifort, grated apple, honey, and lemon juice). Brown toast, butter, and marmalade. Nescafé.

Eleven o'clock: Mackeson stout.

Lunch: Fried mashed potatoes and onions topped with eggs. Fruit (dates or raisins), or cheese and cream crackers.

Cocktail time: Gin or ale.

Dinner: Boiled vegetables—potatoes and onions (enough to fry for lunch the following day). Tinned fish, perhaps Chinook salmon. Bartlett pears.

During the night: Numerous cups of coffee or tea made with a tea bag. Biscuits—ginger nuts a special favourite.

'All the main stores must be on board at Buckler's Hard by May 25th or 26th, before *Gipsy Moth* makes her coastal hop to Plymouth, the final departure point. There, at the last minute, fresh wholemeal bread and fruit will be stowed and Mrs Chichester hopes to make her husband a few salads to see him on his way round the Lizard. On her trip home with him after the 1960 race she made a salad every day of grated carrots, apples, onions, raisins, nuts and lemon juices—"but of course men won't bother to do that".'

The main stores were loaded and stowed by May 26th, and on May 27th Francis left the Beaulieu River for Plymouth, sailing with Sheila Chichester and David Fairhall on board. They reached Plymouth over the weekend, and moored at Cremyll, off the Mashford Brothers' yard. While all the work of fitting-out *Gipsy*, and preparing for the voyage, was going on, at least an equal amount of work went into the organization of her radio communications. In theory, Francis could have picked up his radiotelephone anywhere at sea, and spoken directly to any telephone in England. On trial trips he had made one or two calls to the *Guardian* office in Manchester, and in the first few days of his voyage he spoke to Sheila at their home in London. The idea of receiving messages from *Gipsy* daily in the *Guardian* office was attractive, but there were a number of hazards.

First, if communication was weak, transferring the call to the public telephone system might have lost still more of it. Secondly, handling a radiotelephone call in bad conditions really requires an operator specially trained in marine telephony, so with the help of the Post Office we played safe and arranged to talk to *Gipsy* every day from the GPO's Marine Radio Terminal at Brent. I think that this decision had a lot to do with the final success of the whole operation. Mr S. Gray, the Engineer in Charge at Brent, and the whole staff there, put their hearts into the job of keeping track of *Gipsy*, and at times when conditions were very bad they did whatever may be the radio engineers' equivalent of moving heaven and earth to maintain contact with her. The whole of the vast GPO organization was eager to help this little ship at sea. In the first few days *Gipsy*'s calls went out on medium frequency to Land's End Radio, and from there were transferred by landline to Brent. Later they went out on HF transmissions, and were received at post office stations at Baldock, Herts, Bearly, Warwickshire, and Cooling, Kent. Whichever made the best reception sent the call on to Brent. Communications to *Gipsy* went by landline to Rugby, and went out by radio from there.

Mr Wilson and his staff worked out a kind of immense radio time-map, giving the times in each twenty-four hours that were likely to be most suitable for radio. These were mostly very inconvenient for people, who occasionally like to sleep, for they fell for the most part in the dim hours of the night; but they worked. The *Guardian* side of the telephone at Brent was manned by the brothers David and John Fairhall of the *Guardian* staff, who took their watches much as if they were at sea. The work of the engineers at Brent was not only valuable in obtaining Francis Chichester's narrative from day to day: it was also of material importance to the success of the voyage. From Brent we were able to give Francis Greenwich Mean Time to check his chronometer, and we were also able to send him daily weather reports from the Meteorological Office, and to give him the reported positions of icebergs near his course. The Met. Office, with the particular help of Sir Graham Sutton, the Director General, and Mr B. C. V. Oddie, Deputy Director, did a splendid job in preparing special

B

forecasts for the area of the North Atlantic approximately 100 miles ahead of Francis's last-known position as we gave it them each day. They also collected every scrap of information they could about icebergs, which are a major anxiety to navigators as they approach the Newfoundland coast.

In a big ship equipped with radar, icebergs are a hazard which can be guarded against in the ordinary course of keeping watch, but for a single-handed navigator, who was to sleep, they are the gravest menace on a North Atlantic crossing. The vile early summer helped Francis a bit here, for it had been so cold in the Arctic as well as in England that icebergs broke off late, and did not come so far south as they do in some years. But there were still a few dangerous monsters drifting near his course, and we were able to give him news of most of them—in the event, of all that mattered.

June 1st was a Friday, and by the Monday of that week, May 28th, Francis and *Gipsy Moth III* were at Plymouth, and pretty well ready to start. The last three clear days were spent in getting a few final adjustments made by the Mashford Brothers, and in taking on fresh vegetables and final stores. The night before *Gipsy* sailed, the Lord Mayor of Plymouth, the Rev P. B. ('Tubby') Clayton, Vice-Admiral Sir Conolly Abel Smith and a number of other guests attended a farewell dinner, given in Francis's honour by Colonel Whitbread, who had been a staunch supporter of the venture from the start. Colonel Whitbread is a keen yachtsman, and as an amateur pilot he did a lot of flying in the early days, when Francis was setting up records in the air. A particularly pleasing incident was the presentation to Francis of a flag specially designed by the Institute of Navigation.

The day of departure brought one of the first really fine days of the summer, and Francis crossed the starting line at 1100 hours (BST) in brilliant sunshine, escorted across Plymouth Sound by a noble fleet of little vessels including, I am glad to say, a smart, red Silhouette, *Waskasoo*, sailed by eighty-four-year-old Mr William Spurrell, who is the senior skipper of the Silhouette Register.

As *Gipsy Moth III* passed the breakwater, and stood out to sea, the escorting fleet gradually fell away, leaving him to his long struggle with the Atlantic Ocean alone. To those of us who were there, it was a moving moment. Through the centuries many small ships on great errands have made their departure from Plymouth. *Gipsy Moth III* is among the smallest, but her errand was not the least great.

Of the voyage that followed, Francis's narrative speaks for itself. It will surely rank as one of the great single-handed voyages of all time. He failed to achieve his private ambition of a crossing in thirty days, but he knocked almost a full week—six days and twenty-one hours—off his record time in 1960, and his time of thirty-three days and fifteen hours will stand as a remarkable achievement. Moreover, he devoted much time in the first few weeks to keeping alive a sick homing pigeon, which landed on *Gipsy*, lost and bedraggled, on the second day out from Plymouth. The pigeon was lost overboard on June 21st, and Francis's heroic efforts at rescue, putting about a 13-tonner time and time again single-handed, and keeping track of a tiny pigeon for forty minutes in the vastness of an Atlantic swell, will rank as one of the greatest feats of seamanship of our generation.

The radio achievement of the voyage was also substantial. The failure of the charging engine, installed to provide power for the batteries, the troubles that ensued, and how they were dealt with, are all described in the narrative: the outcome was a great achievement by Francis himself, and by British radio engineering.

A word about my editing: Really, I come into this at all only because Francis was at sea, taking *Gipsy Moth III* back to England, when this book had to be produced. The voyage and the narrative are his. My part has been simply to take his daily pieces, sent by radiotelephone to the *Guardian*, to relate them to his working logs, which he sent me from New York, and to assemble the material into a whole. Anyone who has ever sailed in a small boat—and imagination should be enough for those who have not—will understand that his daily messages to the *Guardian*, and his working logs, had to be prepared in conditions often of great difficulty and discomfort. Therefore, there has been need for some re-arranging to make a connected narrative. But I have added nothing in any material sense, and where some piece of explanation has been needed to explain events, this is made clear in the text. Where I have occasionally re-arranged something, I have been at pains to preserve the integrity of Francis's own writing.

We are indebted to the Editor of the *Guardian* for permission to include much that originally appeared in the *Guardian*'s pages, and I personally owe a great debt to David and John Fairhall for all their work during the actual crossing, and to George Hurley, of Plymouth, for much practical kindness to us all. I must also thank, on Francis's behalf as well as my own, Miss Monica Cooper in London, who typed his handwritten working logs in the shortest possible time, and Miss Mary Walthall in Manchester, who typed the whole manuscript of this book.

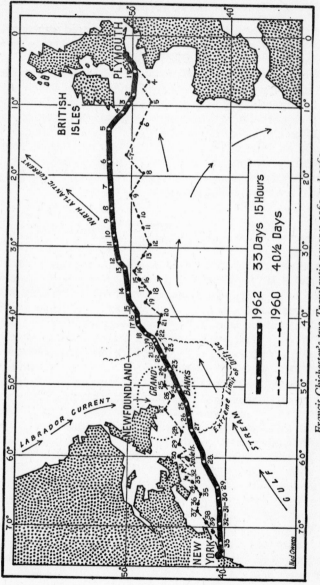

Francis Chichester's two Translantic voyages 1960 and 1962

THE VOYAGE

by Francis Chichester

I

The Start

***

THE drawbacks of racing alone across the Atlantic may be obvious, but what are the advantages, which must be great to make one wish to do it again? Loneliness, which you would think a disadvantage, only lasts for a short period of time, while breaking contact with the land, and for a few hours after that. From then on it seems to me one is only in a long race. I mean, that if you were in a cross-country race you wouldn't worry about being alone, and a trip across the Atlantic is only a longer race. There is the obvious thrill of surging through the Atlantic swell and seas with all sail set, and lovely bow waves combing each side. There is the adventure of 3,000 miles of the Atlantic ahead of you. A voyage is like a classical drama: it starts slowly and works up with many adventurous incidents to the finish.

When I am alone on an adventure I become more efficient. I seem to be twice as efficient, and I become vitalized. I don't know why—perhaps it is because when I am with someone else I am concerned with their comfort or safety rather than getting on with the job. I have always been keen on doing things alone.

When I was a boy I used to wander all day through the woods in north Devon by myself. I used to go bird-nesting, but only to get a single egg from some particularly difficult buzzard's nest, or crow's nest.

One day, when I was about eleven, I caught a viper. I thought it might be hungry, and I showed it a beetle which I thought would make a good meal. It hissed, and bit me instead. For twenty hours or so, I was told, it was touch and go whether I would survive. Perhaps I made things worse by the fact that I travelled seven miles as fast as I could running, and on a bicycle, hampered for the first part of the journey by the snake that I was still carrying. Perhaps this adventure with the snake ought to have taught me a lesson in sticking to the job: if I'd killed the snake instead of trying to please it, none of this trouble would have arisen. But I did try to please the snake, and got bitten for it. When you are quite alone you don't have to think about pleasing anybody, or anything else. You can give your whole being to the job in hand, and there is immense pleasure in using manual dexterity.

When on a solo adventure, it seems to me that all one's sensations are magnified: the sensation of excitement, the feeling of accomplishment, of fear perhaps, or of pleasure. All one's senses are more acute. One sees and preceives more the beauty and details of the sky and the water, their colour or shape. One's touch is more sensitive, and the feeling of water and wind and things become more real and more acute. One tastes things more sharply; everything tastes better, or worse, than usual. One's hearing is more acute. One becomes so tuned up that the slightest change of conditions, of weather, or noise, or movement will be perceived and, in fact, will wake one up after being alone for a while. Another curious thing about prolonged solitude is that time seems to change its rate. Sometimes there seems a long interval between two words you are thinking, as if you dropped them separately into a pool; sometimes when you are in some difficult situation time goes incredibly fast, sometimes incredibly slowly. Time's values change.

Apart from boyhood adventures in north Devon, my first big adventures alone were with mechanical power in the air, when I flew *Gipsy Moth I* solo from England to Australia in 1929, and made the first east-west solo flight from New Zealand to Australia across the Tasman Sea. A voyage in sail has advantages over a flight because you are using natural forces, the wind and water, for your power, instead of mechanical power. Secondly, you are using more physical effort, and this always results in more pleasure than a nervous effort. Thirdly, because a voyage in sail takes longer, the experience is more protracted.

My solo transatlantic passage in 1962 was very different from the 1960 one. There is no magic like the first-time adventure: the second time you know it can be done, so bang goes a lot of romance. Romance is an exciting adventure into the unknown, as I see it.

This year it was still a big adventure, but of a different kind. Chiefly, it was a formidable project in this way: I came out into the open and declared I would start on June 1st to cross the Atlantic, that I aimed to beat my 1960 forty-day record, and lastly that I was trying to do it in thirty days.

In the early days of flying we used to be scared to disclose even a destination, not to speak of an ETA; it invited bad luck, if not disaster. So the great battle for me this year was against time. Every ocean racer is acutely aware of the 100 things that can prevent a yacht from reaching the starting line. Family affairs for the skipper, crew trouble, broken gear, being hit by another vessel, stranding or grounding, for example. I reached the line on time, one deep breath of relief. Now I wanted to cut out 3,000 miles in thirty days. But before I got to the line much had to be done. I started living on board *Gipsy* in the Beaulieu River in March, and we had our first sail under her new rig one Sunday towards the end of April.

We did not get away from the mooring until two o'clock in the afternoon, after church, and a visit to *Gipsy Moth* by Tubby Clayton with one of his disciples (or ADCs ?). Now as to our trials. First, concerning Miranda II, the Mark II version of my self-steering vane. The sail was cut two inches too long in the leech instead of dead flat. As a result it flapped badly in anything of a wind. A bottle-screw on one of the wire stays to the end of the boom quickly shook itself free and disappeared into the Solent. That I soon replaced by a lanyard. Maybe this floppy sail was a good thing: it showed up weaknesses bound to give trouble in a storm. I decided to add two long battens and two rows of reefing eyes, as well as getting the sail flat. It was also clear that Miranda's mast would have to be strengthened greatly. The flapping sail made the mast whip and shake below the sleeve. I decided to get Ian Proctor's advice about it.

We ran down the Solent dead before the wind under Miranda's control, which never could be done before because of the backstay's interference with the vane. That old backstay has been changed to twin backstays farther forward, allowing Miranda to swing right round. The new Miranda is more powerful too. Also partly due to Miranda, *Gipsy Moth* did well on a broad reach, only hunting through an arc of 30 degrees instead of through 90 degrees as before. But this was partly due to the new rig by John Illingworth, as a result of which *Gipsy Moth* is well balanced and easier to control.

Unfortunately, the old mainsail, recut to the new look, had come out wrong. It was too baggy. This was something that had to be cured: it could not be endured.

While all this work of adjustment and making new fittings went on, I had some more sailing. I remember particularly one day when I finished lunch at eleven p.m., and dropped into my berth at midnight. It was only a voyage to Cowes and back, about eight miles each way. I had wanted to take my Miranda sail there for more alterations, because it still would not fit. I had meant to leave my mooring in the Beaulieu River at eight, but I didn't get away until eleven a.m. It always amazes me the number of jobs to be done on a 13-ton boat before one can sail, and as I had to moor up on the trots at Cowes single-handed, I had to prepare four fenders and two warps. I got three sails bent and cast off the mooring. It was one of those lovely spring mornings with an occasional cuckoo and a romantic freshness of tone, a few gulls mewing, and later thousands of them squalling in their nests along the spit. The sun shone hot, but it was cold out of it with an ENE. breeze. I trimmed up the new No. 2 jib (which I was trying out for the first time) with a staysail and the main until the boat sailed itself for a while.

But when I had crossed the Solent hard on the wind, I lost a lot of ground to the westward with the strong 2½-3 knot tide stream against me, the wind against me, and only a light breeze at that, so I had to spoil the lovely scene by starting the motor. I switched off and sailed when the breeze freshened a little. Off the Squadron Castle at Cowes the time came for me to lower the sails. All went well with the headsails, but the reel winch on which the mainsail wire halliard was wound, like thread on a reel, jammed and refused to budge. The reel was partly off its spindle. I tried to free it, banged it with a wooden mallet, but it would not budge. There was a nice fix, with the main jammed up and no bosun's chair rig with which I could haul myself up to the top of the 50-foot mast. In the end I found I could work the wire off the reel a turn at a time between the reel and the guard designed to prevent the wire from doing just that thing.

I bustled off with Miranda's sail and her 11-foot spar, and Sherlaws were soon putting it right. This took time, and it was six p.m. when I emerged from the Medina River. The tide stream now turned and was really strong against me again, but I thought it would be all right with a nice easterly breeze astern to waft me home. No such luck; the breeze had gone round to west. With a $3\frac{1}{2}$-knot stream off Cowes I should be carried halfway to Portsmouth if I tried to cross there.

Either I must wait until the tide turned favourable in the Solent at nine-thirty (when, however, it would be against me all the 4 miles up the Beaulieu River) or else put the motor on and creep round the point at Cowes with sails flapping. Purist yachting men, forgive me; I motored and flapped. The motor was making a horrible row, and I was forced to realize that the exhaust pipe was leaking. When I had crept far enough up the coast of the island, I tacked and headed for the mainland, sailing. I switched off and tried to repair the exhaust pipe (which I feared would set the boat on fire) by strapping it with a Whitbread Pale Ale can (after I had suitably emptied it).

As soon as I got into the river the breeze began to die on me, and I switched on the motor again. After a while the cylinder belching into that exhaust pipe stopped firing. I held on for a while, busy with navigating in the narrow channel, hoping it would pick up firing again. When I looked into the cabin it was invisible for sooty black smoke. I switched off, threw out a charred piece of wood, and hurriedly loosened the kedge anchor and dropped it just before *Gipsy Moth* charged her favourite mudbank. Balked of her evil desire, she strained against the kedge, still pointing at the bank. The kedge warp rubbed off green anti-fouling paint under the bottom. I hoisted the mainsail, and finally coaxed *Gipsy Moth* into a heading so that I could free and haul aboard the anchor and get back to the tiller before the yacht charged the bank. I began tacking to and fro across the channel in a zephyr, but the tide was making slowly up river—in my favour for the first time that day. The zephyr became imperceptible, but still *Gipsy Moth* ghosted on over the reflection of the western sky where the huge red sun was dropping behind the trees. The water was glassy. In the end the yacht swung across the river in a dead calm, then a faint puff took her aback and she headed for the bank. Our wills tangled. I did not want her to hit the mud and lie on her side all night. I dropped into the dinghy astern like a rabbit out of a hat, after running along the deck with a warp from the stem. I rowed hard and tugged at the reluctant stem standing black in the still water. Slowly she came round and headed upstream. The dinghy jerked to a halt; the warp flicked taut; the yacht moved slowly. After half a mile a man coming along in a dinghy with a motor offered me a pluck, and I accepted with a little regret; it appealed to me then, the prospect of towing *Gipsy Moth* through Buckler's Hard to her mooring with an 8-foot dinghy.

Another mile would have done it. One man, a stranger, called out to me: 'You can't imagine how lovely her reflection looks, black in the water.' That was how I came to have lunch at eleven p.m. on the first day of May.

I used to think it extraordinary to read of ships of the line taking months to fit out for a voyage; I no longer do. Even in this 13-tonner there always seem to be a thousand things to service, to make ready, or to make work. And I have no seventy-four guns to attend to, only one modest Very pistol which merely has to be cleaned and oiled, and its cartridges checked, so many red and white flares. I suppose that the rockets I carry and the red and white flares are nearly in the gunpowder class. Slowly I got through the items on my agenda, making it seem possible that I could be ready for the deep sea one day soon. Yet the list seemed endless. There was the compass to be adjusted, with sundry moorings and anchorings down river. This turned out well, with no disturbance in north and south headings, which is nice, only in east and west. I like a good compass position with little deviation to correct.

Then there were the anchors to be bedded down in the starboard berth in the forecabin. I first chose the sites carefully where they would take up least room, and then I drilled for twenty screws to secure the ten metal chocks to keep them in place in heavy weather. Then I rigged tackles into the staysail sheets, which I thought would be an improvement on winches for single-handed work. Next I rigged a curtain over the entrance to the cabin; the three washboards which drop into slots to close the entrance and stand up to a big sea are excellent, but they are an obstruction to quick exits and entrances. And there was the engine, which had given trouble and reduced me to despair by black exhaust carbon from leaking exhaust pipes. I suppose I really resent motors in a sailing vessel. Why have them, you say? Well, without the auxiliary I should have to wait for a favourable tide to get back to my mooring in the Beaulieu River. You can't tack a 40-foot boat against the wind in a narrow channel single-handed, for long. A mainsail alone won't drive her fast enough and tacking a big head sail every minute or so will soon exhaust a single-hander. And the channel at low water is not much wider than the yacht length in places where piles have been driven into the river for mooring. Martin fixed my motor. He runs a garage, and used to look after Lord Montagu's museum of old cars. His fixing of my motor, and of the charging engine, made a big difference. Still, all the time I felt how happy I should be when the boat actually became a sailing vessel again.

The start on June 1st did not go according to plan—I was nearly late across the line. *Gipsy Moth* was at Mashford's Yard, because we had saved up a lot of repairs for them to do. One reason we were there is that Sid Mashford has a wonderful eye for a yacht and any detail on it. No transatlantic yachtsman should leave without letting him have a look at his boat. For example, he found that the pulpit wasn't properly fastened. He also pointed out that a lot of the anti-fouling on the hull was missing, although it was only put on two months before. Another thing he did for me was to show how the lifelines could be better placed, and altogether I felt really confident when I left. At nine a.m. I had gone on board and was preparing to sail. I was just getting things in order when a big launch came alongside and two Customs men stepped aboard. They had just heard that I had a tape-recorder, so they looked all over it, cut open the battery-box and looked at all the batteries, cut open the tape-box and looked at all the tapes. I don't know what they expected to find. I was stamping about on deck, and as a result of the delay we nearly missed the start. While Sid Mashford stowed gear below, my wife took the helm and we rushed down to the line, where my passengers transferred to the harbourmaster's launch. Instead of being calm, and resolute, and all set to do some lovely manoeuvres before the start, there I was in a hurry. I had been told that the forecast promised a north-east wind up to Force 6. Very cautious, as usual, I set the number two jib, but hadn't gone more than a few hundred yards when I found that we had not got enough canvas. So I set my biggest jib, but there still wasn't enough, and I added the staysail.

As I got clear of the breakwater the wind came in from astern and I thought I was in for this north-easter. So I boomed out the genoa. But this was no sooner done than the wind veered and I had to get the 21-foot pole in again. The wind veered once more and the boat was hard on the wind. At Polperro I tacked for the first time. For the rest of that first day I seemed to be re-setting sails all day. The wind was all over the place, but never from the north-east, never.

At six p.m., when I made my first telephone call to the *Guardian*, *Gipsy Moth* was still 15 miles from the Lizard, and we were making only 5 knots. But still—that's yachting.

I found that I hadn't yet got the single-handed attitude of mind: I kept popping up into the cockpit to see what was happening, whereas I should have been content to stay below. But I knew that I would soon tune in to the ocean and its atmosphere, and be happy to listen, and feel for any change in conditions.

II

A Pigeon Joins the Ship

I SPENT the rest of that first evening stowing clothes and gear below, and around nine-thirty I met a fishing boat. The tide turned in my favour at the Lizard about then, and I set a course clear of the Runnelstone, which is a buoy just south of Land's End. I was nearly becalmed in the lee of the Lizard, and the coastguard there flashed me a signal asking me what ship I was. I was nearly becalmed in the lee of Land's End as well. I had no sleep up to then, because I couldn't sleep so close to land, with so many ships about, and also the wind was too variable: if I left the self-steering gear in charge and went to sleep near the land, a slight change of wind direction might have put me ashore. But I couldn't complain: it was a lovely scene, a sort of yachtsman's dream, with clusters of fishing boats, quite brightly lit. I had the red sector of the Wolf Rock to guide me, and I was soon rounding the Runnelstone. Then I got into the red sector of the Longships light off Land's End. This made me think of Ann Davison in her story *Last Voyage*, and I became convinced that this was the 'baleful red light' that she could not identify. After I left Land's End you might think that I was clear, but I still had the Seven Stones to avoid, a cluster of rocks north-west of Land's End, with a lightship there.

I was getting very sleepy indeed, so I decided to have a sleep, and I set an alarm clock for an hour and a half later, which I reckoned would give me a safety margin of time in case the wind changed and was bearing me down on the rocks. But a nice breeze got up, and *Gipsy Moth* was heeled over twenty-five degrees and I got my decks well washed. It was rather thrilling to be at sea again, and to hear the water gurgling and swishing outside the hull, alongside my ear while I lay in my bunk. We were being bumped about a bit, but all the same a red carnation, placed in a glass on my swinging table by my cousin Myra before I left, stayed in the glass. When I woke up I found that the wind had held, and we were well north of the Seven Stones. Then I turned in properly, and had a fairly good sleep from three a.m. until about nine o'clock. To show what a good breeze we had, we did forty-four miles in seven and a half hours, an average of nearly six knots. But I was woken at 9 o'clock by the sails flapping in a calm, and I began working hard to try to get more speed out of the yacht. I boomed out my No. 2 jib, so that I had 1,090 square feet of sail set. In spite of that I managed to get only seven and a half miles in three hours. Then we were nearly becalmed again, and *Gipsy* went round twice in a slow circle. There was some awful rolling, but it was lovely sunny weather, with the sun hot and only fair weather clouds in the sky.

After I had my morning Mackeson I had a delicious salad lunch, made from some salad given me by Mrs Odling-Smee, wife of the former Rear-Commodore of the Royal Western Yacht Club. I felt absolutely on top of the world, and I was almost tempted to jump overboard to have a swim; but I did some work on board instead, trimming sails, and trying to charge the batteries. I ran the generator for three and three-quarter hours, but the batteries were still not fully charged. I also contrived to lose the funnel for filling the generator in the bilge.

Miranda, my self-steering vane, controlled the yacht even when I could not tell where the faint air was coming from, helping her to ghost along quietly, too slowly for the log to register. This was a wonderful success for the new model Miranda, and couldn't have been achieved with the old one. But calm is no fun at all for a sailor: the boom sways to and fro and the whole yacht shakes when it comes up against the sheets; blocks creak and sails flap. In one period of ten hours I did only ten miles. Finally, I took down the mainsail to spare it the hard time it was having as it slatted about, and then of course there was nothing to prevent the yacht from rolling, which she did in no uncertain terms. But I still did not feel like complaining. I never had a day's weather like this in the whole of the 1960 race. The sun shone out of a cloudless sky, and there was a lovely dark blue sea, and it gave me a chance to catch up on stowage and getting jobs done. Another great compensation was that I got a wonderful sleep, pyjamas, nylon sheets, and all.

The great event of my second day at sea was the arrival of Pidgy, a handsome homing pigeon, which I found underneath a sail on the foredeck. It is a great event for a single-handed sailor when a bird comes on board. Pidgy was very diffident, and I could not catch him, but he was intensely curious and seemed to want to know exactly what I was doing. He kept perching on the companionway to see what I was doing in the cabin. As I was tuning up my radio to talk to the *Guardian*, Billy Cotton suddenly came through with that show of his. Pidgy perched on the chart table to listen to it. Soon after I first found Pidgy, I gave him some muesli and water, which he seemed to enjoy, but afterwards I had great difficulty in persuading him to eat. I tried him with all sorts of food, salad, oatmeal, and everything I could think of, but he didn't seem very keen on any of it. I think he was seasick: he looked terrible, all fluffed up, bleary-eyed, and with his head tucked under his wing. I wondered whether he would last the night, but in the morning he seemed to revive.

He still wouldn't eat, but he kept on following me about. He looked very sick to me. He was certainly not house-trained, but I didn't grudge it him. But he did make a frightful mess. When I was sunbathing on deck he jumped into the cabin, and when I discovered him he had already made a frightful mess on the cabin sole. Thank heaven it was not on the carpet. I had to follow him round the boat with a bucket. He did eat some food at last, and I made a box for him in the cockpit, giving him a mallet and a piece of rope to stand on. I thought that I could probably sell the guano rights on that mallet for a large sum when I got to America! But Pidgy must be about the most stupid pigeon ever. He kept on pecking like mad at a saucer he finished long ago, but wouldn't look at the new supply I put in his box and showed to him several times.

Note: The pigeon which took refuge on Gipsy Moth *was identified by the National Homing Union from the letters and figures on his ring, which Francis Chichester gave to the* Guardian *by radio-telephone. He was a cock, belonging to Mr Arthur Banks, a nursery-man, of Marsh Lane, Longton, near Preston, bred from a distinguished pair of racing parents in what Mr Banks described as 'a long-distance French family'. In 1961 he finished fifth in a race from Guernsey to Longton—the Longton Two Bird Open. He was released in the Channel Islands to take part in the race this year on the day after Chichester left Plymouth, and was apparently blown off his course, to land exhausted on Gipsy's foredeck. Francis was much concerned about the pigeon's exhausted state, and very much bothered when he could not persuade it to eat. He asked us on the Guardian whether we could get him some expert advice about pigeons, and we sought advice from the Curator of Birds at the London Zoo, the RSPCA, and the Severn Wildfowl Trust. All responded readily, and suggested much the kind of food that he was already giving it—nuts, oatmeal, and broken biscuit. They also advised fresh greenstuff, and Francis gave the pigeon what he had, but fresh greenstuff on a small sailing boat well out to sea is not easy to come by.—J.R.L.A.*

The next day, June 4th, was a tremendous contrast to the day before. Then, I was sunbathing on top of the cabin, lying on a sail and telling myself that I could not remember the weather ever having been so good during a race. This morning I was doing my office work at the chart table when I heard a loud bang. I rushed on deck to find that a rope grommet holding the 21-foot spinnaker pole to the clew of the genoa had parted in a gale squall. That meant a lot of trouble: there was a 420-square-foot jib blowing about in a Force 8 wind. I had to work very hard to get it in with the other big genoa too—maybe I shouldn't have carried them so long, but it was good sport running down from the Fastnet in such a wind. It took me two or three hours to get the sails in and secured; now and again seas came aboard which made things difficult with the yacht dancing about. I worked away steadily and got the storm jib up, and then the spitfire (another small, tough jib) on the foretopmast stay. Just with these I did a merry 6 knots. But all this was rather too much for Miranda, whose vane works through a band brake, which began slipping.

That didn't make things any easier. Just before noon I tried to take a sextant shot, but was interrupted by a steamer, which came and circled round me, asking if I wanted any help. I had to wait until he had gone before I could get down to things again, but I

C

did get a noon position, and it put me 51° 34′ N., 11° 00′ W. This gave me 119 miles made good in twenty-four hours, and 290 miles altogether.

It was a rolling, twisting ride in the Atlantic, but after I had finished setting my storm jibs I would have enjoyed it if I had not been feeling rather sick. I had some trouble getting through on the radiotelephone—London could not hear me, although I could hear them. Afterwards I found a sail tie touching the lead in through the deck, which may have been the reason. In the evening I decided to set the trysail, but after I had set and trimmed it, I found that it interfered with the staysail, so I downed that. The sea was growing, and *Gipsy Moth* was flung from side to side, but moving fast under trysail and working jib. I had a successful radiotelephone call to the *Guardian* late that night, and immediately afterwards felt tired and turned in. I went to sleep, but was soon woken up by the sails roaring, *Gipsy*'s rough ride across the seas, and the wind. When I saw the tell-tale compass in the cabin that she was 60° off course, I got up, dressed in oilies, and went back to work.

In the small hours I had much trouble with the steering, for Miranda was slipping badly. I calmed things down, and then took a piece of wire and slipped it into the brake band to tighten it. It seemed to work. The pigeon squatted on the cockpit seat in a corner, and took no notice when I stepped right alongside him. Poor devil, he must have been feeling awful. I, too, felt sick, and had some hot water and sugar. I tried to turn in again, but it was difficult to sleep for noise and movement, so I went out again to re-secure the main boom, and to let water out of the cockpit.

With morning, the wind went down a bit, though it was still strong, and I still felt sick. There was a squall just before noon, gusting up to 60 m.p.h., which meant more work with the sails, and much trimming of Miranda. I felt the need of a smaller Miranda for gales. The wind was blowing around Force 6 to 7 from the south, and I had several waves over me; water ran up my trouser legs, into the top of the long boots inside them. I decided to double reef Miranda, which was a difficult, dirty, and tricky job in that sea, standing on the afterdeck. But it was well worth it, for instead of banging, flapping, jerking and not working, Miranda's sail fell happily asleep.

Then I took on another longish job of setting the spitfire on the foretopmast stay, but that also was well worth it, for the ship began going really well in the right direction, and quietly. Of course seas still picked her up and threw her on to her side, or slewed her round, sometimes her counter, sometimes her head. I had no luck with the radio, but just got through enough to say to Land's End that my aerial was awash with heavy seas, and to give my position.

Around six o'clock an RAF Shackleton came over, making passes. It was overcast and misty, with poor visibility of only a mile or so. The wind was Force 6, gusting to 8. The Shackleton did well to find me in that muck. I went up to see them; I must have looked pretty wet without oilies. They must have thought me unresponsive.

Pidgy seemed to have disappeared. Earlier on, a sea had washed him off the counter, and he had to take to the air. I thought he'd gone then, but after circling several times, he came back again. I don't know where he hid after that, but he turned up again in the night. He looked all in, but he showed a wonderful sense of balance, swaying to the roll without looking; and he had no hand to hold on by. He just stood on a slat of the cockpit seat.

Note: This was the worst day for communication in the whole of Chichester's passage. He was then at one of the most difficult stages of his trip, from the radio point of view—almost too far away for medium frequency communication with the coastal station at Land's End, and not far enough for good long range communication by HF. *But by some really brilliant work, Land's End Radio did manage to pick him up, and pass on to the* Guardian *the essential information giving his position, and a few words about the rough time he was having.—J.R.L.A.*

III

Trouble

THE weather was still foul, but I had a good sleep from ten p.m. until around one-thirty a.m., when I was woken up by a class I shemozzle. I found the sails aback, and the yacht heading east— back the way we had come. The cord fastening a side block for Miranda's tiller line had parted, and unfortunately I had some elastic shock cord helping the tiller to windward, and the shock cord took charge. We took no harm, and thank heaven it was no worse. I dealt with the situation, and I had just dried off and got rid of my oilies, when there was more trouble, which I found was due to the block on the other tiller line breaking away. So I put on oilies again and went through everything else again. I went on to the foredeck to look at the sail trim, and conditions certainly were rugged. It was hard to keep a hold, even using both hands, and there were deluges of sea. Pidgy, in the locker under the cockpit seat, was very bedraggled and sick-looking. I feared for his life, but there seemed nothing much that I could do for him.

I decided that I might as well try to get some more sleep, and I did manage to doze from sometime after three a.m. until about eight a.m. I awoke to a drizzle of rain, with mist keeping visibility to little more than 300 yards or so, but the wind had moderated to around Force 5, and the sea was moderating too. But big seas occasionally threw the yacht over.

I worked hard that morning (June 6th). First, I cleared the bilges, and pumped them out with thirty-seven pulls at the pump. Then I exchanged a few sentences on the radiotelephone with London. I tried leading the aerial directly to the set from the companion, but they said it was better the other way, through the insulator, although it was dripping water through the cabin top on to the chart table. We arranged to have another try later. I had breakfast off Kenco coffee (darned good) and muesli (ditto). Then

I made Pidgy a hut in the port side forward locker under the forward seat by putting a Cellophane roof over the top. I put a dish of Macvita and bread inside, plus a bowl of fresh water, both of which he went for. He seemed better than he had been during the night. Perhaps, like me, he felt less seasick.

Then I got to work trying to charge the batteries, but the generator ran for only five minutes. Every time the yacht heeled to starboard it robbed the carburettor of petrol. I felt that I must provide some solution to this, as we should probably be mostly on that tack. After struggling with the generator I got down the spitfire and set the working jib in its place. I got some sousers over me while I was working forward, but my new nylon-PVC suit was damned good.

I spent a lot of time trimming sails, but I could not get them satisfying; they just would not give enough speed. I decided that *Gipsy* could stand a mainsail, so I downed the trysail. But the main halliard had wound itself round a crosstree, so I hoisted the main on the trysail halliard. The result seemed satisfactory. Then I got the big genoa in its bag out of the cabin, though with much difficulty in lifting it through the hatch because of its weight and bulk, and the yacht's heel.

I had an idea about the generator, and got to work to try it out. The trouble seemed to be that the carburettor was starved of petrol when *Gipsy* heeled, so I thought that if I could raise the level of petrol in the tank it might make things better. I got the end off the ensign staff, bored a hole through the middle, and fitted it into the petrol filler opening of the charging motor. This raised the level of petrol. I got a mouthful of petrol in the process— Shell probably tastes better than any other, but still! After all this work I found that it was still no go: The motor died with each big heel, when the petrol (I suppose) swished up to the other end of the reservoir.

In spite of these troubles I felt better, thank heaven, than I had felt for some time. My morning sail trim held good and we galloped through the disturbed sea. The pigeon seemed particularly stupid: he stood on the edge of his plate, and emptied all the food into the cockpit water on the floor. I get pretty stupid when I am seasick, so I sympathized with him really.

In the evening I had a good talk on the radiotelephone to David Fairhall in London, and afterwards I was sitting down below feeling pretty tired when I suddenly noticed from the 'tell-tale' compass that everything was going haywire; we had gone right off course. I pulled my sea-boots towards me, pretty well full of water, but I had to wear them, and I had started putting them on before I tumbled to the cause of the trouble. I had been given a tin of shortbread by a Scots chap in the office, and I suddenly thought of this tin and moved it away. Sure enough, it had somehow become very highly magnetized, and had driven the tell-tale compass round, making me think that we were right off course.

I slept until about two-thirty a.m., and then got up and trimmed Miranda. The wind had dropped. I started the charging motor, but it stopped after fifteen minutes and spluttered all the time. I thought that I had better examine the plug, but I knew that the trouble was definitely connected with rolling. I wondered if the exhaust exit was going under water? I thought that I would set more sail, but a puff of strong wind advised caution. I felt tired and capable of making silly mistakes, so I determined to wait until morning, and we went on with a humble 4 knots.

After the morning's work I got the charging motor going again by pouring an extra quart of petrol through the wooden block. Then it stopped, with a great squealing and squeaking. I tried the flywheel, but it would not budge, so I could only infer that it had seized up.

Note: David Fairhall telephoned me at home that night to say that he had bad news: Francis had just come through on the radiotelephone with a call that might very well be the last; he had reported that the charging motor had seized, and that it was completely out of commission. This was grim, for unless the batteries could be charged, our hopes of keeping radio contact with Francis would end. But there was one faint chance: Gipsy Moth III still had her ordinary auxiliary engine, a Coventry Victor, and this incorporated a small generator, like that in a motor car, for charging the self-starter and lighting batteries. I thought of this, but Francis had already thought of it, for David reported that he was going to see if he could use it for charging the radio batteries. It seemed a pretty desperate hope, for the Coventry Victor only had a twelve-volt dynamo, whereas the radio batteries required twenty-four volts. Still, it might be possible to split and parallel the Exide radio batteries and charge them in two banks. But all this would be a most intricate job, and we were none of us at all sure whether it could be done. In the early hours next morning I got hold of Mr Maconachie of Marconi Marine at Chelmsford, explained the position to him, and asked him to put the problem to Marconi's technical men. I then telephoned Mr C. P. Melly, General Sales Manager of the Coventry Victor Company, and again explained the problem. He and his people at Coventry were all sympathetic, and keen to help. During that morning we assembled all the technical advice we could to pass on to Francis by radiotelephone. He needed power from his batteries mainly for transmitting, and he could use his radio receiver to listen to us with the expenditure of very little current. So we were able to pass on long and detailed messages to him without imperilling the precious charge remaining in his batteries. The Coventry Victor is a marine propulsion engine which, of course, Francis was not using because Gipsy was making the crossing wholly under sail. And he could not use it as it was designed to be used without disqualifying himself from the whole adventure. The problem, therefore, was to find some way of persuading the Victor to run for long periods in neutral, doing nothing but provide charge. Both engine and dynamo were quite unsuitable for this: the engine, like all working engines, worked best under load, and the dynamo was a non-ventilated Lucas generator of the type used in motor cars—excellent for its own job of keeping up the starting battery and providing power for lights, but not at all intended to provide a charge for the big Exides needed for the radiotelephone. To get any charge at all from the Coventry Victor, Francis had first to change the connections of the radio batteries to make them into two parallel banks of twelve-volt units, and this alone was a tricky business in a small sailing boat in an Atlantic seaway—particularly when the man doing it was alone on board, and had to do everything else as well. The Coventry Victor engine in Gipsy is below the cabin sole, well and conveniently placed as an auxiliary engine for being out of the way, but in an extremely awkward position for long and intricate work at sea. Everything was difficult, and gave a great deal of trouble. Francis got his connections made and then ran into the problem of overheating when he tried to run the engine for long periods in a way it was never designed for. He stuck at all this with the calm, determined toughness that is characteristic of him, and somehow or other he made things work. To the end of the voyage the Marconi 'Kestrel' set went on transmitting, and we never missed a day's reception. Quite why things worked remains more in the category of miracle than of mechanical or electrical engineering, but they did work. This success seems to me an immense tribute, not only to Francis, but to all the British products concerned—the radio set itself, the Coventry Victor engine, and the Exide batteries. They could not have been asked to work in worse conditions; they were abused, and made to do things that their designers would have shuddered at; but they worked, and went on working.—J.R.L.A.

IV

Ups and Downs

TWICE in the night I woke up to find that we were pointing the wrong way. We had swung round in a calm, and since I didn't want to go east I had to get up and trim the boat. I finally got up to have breakfast at six a.m., and just as I was sitting down to eat something, I saw that we were heading north-east again. I thought it was Miranda's fault, but it wasn't her at all: in a few minutes the wind had swung from south-west to north. I straightened things out, and went over on the starboard tack, the first change of tack for five or six days. There was very little wind, perhaps Force 1, but we ghosted along fairly well. I took the opportunity of the calm to tackle several days of washing up, and to deal with arrears of shaving and personal ablution. I got a sun shot at noon (June 8th) and found that we had made good a total of 762 miles towards New York. The log seemed to be persistently under-reading. Partly this was because of the periods of *Gipsy*'s ghosting, when we moved through the water too slowly to move the log, but there was more to be accounted for than that. I looked into things thoroughly, and discovered the trouble: the bearings were sticking. Moreover, the strain had made the line kink a good deal between the lead and the spinner. It is quite hard to train a log properly. The instructions say, 'Don't oil', but I gave it a good oiling, and after that it seemed to be running well. Next, I fitted Miranda with a cordage so that it could be put into action by pulling the cord from the cockpit. I tried fixing a bamboo to the lever with another cord on the other side to disengage the clutch, but the bamboo broke and I didn't have anything suitable to use instead.

When I am alone at sea I don't have much time to get lonely: one is fully occupied in doing one's job. I felt very fit, but I was feeling a bit tired. I hadn't had all the sleep I needed: in bad weather, when I was being thrown about, I couldn't sleep properly, and tended to wake up feeling more tired than when I went to sleep. But fatigue is accepted as the great enemy to ocean racing.

In the evening I had a talk with Cliff Michelmore, and Sheila, for the BBC's 'Tonight' television programme, and then a long talk with Mr Gray (the Engineer in Charge at Brent) about my batteries, and the main motor. I had to think things out hard. One thing I had to do to save electricity was to get out my oil lamps and candles. It was quite like old times.

Pidgy looked very old and dark, and sick, and his behaviour was terrible: I had to mop up after him before I could step in the cockpit, or on the counter. He never seemed to learn about eating, and always stepped on the side of his dish, and upset it.

Late that night I managed to connect the main engine to the Marconi batteries, and ran the motor for sixteen and a half minutes. But the generator got hot, and so did the gear-case. I decided to leave things for the moment, and think about it all tomorrow.

With morning, June 9th, we were still becalmed: I freed Miranda and lashed the helm. What wind there was switched 180 degrees to the south, and kept me mucking about on deck. I tacked and set Miranda when a puff came, but it was only a zephyr. The cockpit, with all Miranda's gear, looked like a tangle of cobwebs: I don't know what Sheila would have said about it! I decided to turn in again for a bit in the hope that the wind would have decided what to do when I woke up.

I slept very well until eight-thirty a.m., but found the wind still around Force 1, with the sea calm, and a slight swell. There was a red slit on the horizon, above the sun's position, but it was slightly overcast. We had done 10½ miles in eight hours. One big event was that Pidgy gave tongue to a small 'roucou roucou'. He seemed a bit more cheerful, doing some eagle antics, flapping his wings, and hopping on to the crosstree.

I worked hard on the main engine. It was an awkward situation, face down under the cockpit, and I only just survived seasickness. I unfastened the bolt securing the gear lever, because I thought that the lever had not enough play. I found that the propeller shaft had reversed itself at slow revs, and then switched to the other rotation on opening the throttle. I secured the shaft with a piece of very old cod line. This is one use for which nylon is no good—that is, to supply a hold which will break at once if too much strain is applied to it. It worked, so I felt ready to start trying to charge the batteries, but the wind got up a little, so I decided to defer charging until a bit later.

I also felt like lunch, and I had a splendid lunch, eating the last lettuce given me by Nancy, which was excellent with a crushed garlic clove. One advantage of the Atlantic is that one can eat as much garlic and onion as one likes, and I like a lot. I had smoked salmon first, but it was too salt, packed in brine, with Danish Blue cheese, and gingerbread to follow. I made a blunder here; I didn't have Stilton as I had last time; Stilton just has that extra something. I had dates and raisins in my salad and, of course, a Mackeson stout to start with, and Whitbread pale ale to go on with. The *tout ensemble* would be hard to beat.

I decided to alter my clocks: one feels that one had been wasting time, lunching at three p.m., whereas actually it is not local noon here until two-forty British clock time.

Later that afternoon we had a shower of rain, and the wind quickened. I made another tent for Pidgy on the cockpit seat leaning to the coaming at one end. It had macintosh sheets (at least, their modern equivalent, a Cellophane bag folded flat). But I found that I couldn't see him in this position, so I shifted the tent to the other end of the cockpit, facing forward. He was more out of my way there too.

Sailing was getting much better, and we were moving fast. It is a fine sensation to be sailing fast through the smoothest ocean sea, and to watch the waves and white water seeming to rush past the cabin portholes.

In the evening we had a squall, with rain and wind, but not much sea. We were going so fast that we bounced, but I hung on, although over-canvassed, because I thought it was only temporary and anyway we were doing 6 to 7 knots. The yacht went through one or two waves without slowing, but it was surprising to see how, if she came to a succession of waves, her jumping developed a certain rhythm, so would slow right down.

I lacked judgement in thinking that the wind was only a short rain squall. It took me a long time to get the sails reset—an hour and twenty-five minutes. What took most of the time was sorting out the halliards, which were all crossed because of being one winch short (and my clumsiness). I handed my genoa, reefed Miranda, reefed the main, and set the working jib. Under working jib, staysail, and reefed main, we were going at least as fast as before, with the wind coming from the south-west at about Force 6. The sea bumped a cupful of tea leaves and some tea off the swinging table on to the carpet. Poor carpet. It was getting more off-white daily. I said to myself, 'What ho! for a Squire's gin and lemon hot.' Then I hardened in the main, and turned in. Just before midnight I had to turn out again, because we were taking too big a pounding. I got down the working jib, and set the storm jib in its place, getting well dunked in the process.

That was an uncomfortable night. I had to get up again at two-thirty when the wind dropped and I was awoken because the boom was banging in too little wind. I took some waking, but I had to get to work again—to get down the spitfire, to set the big genoa, and to unreef the main. I tacked to the SSE., but it was no good, so I tacked back. There followed much trimming in a light wind, and for some reason I seemed temporarily to lose my sense of balance, and couldn't walk along the deck without holding on all the time, which was a nuisance. Day broke (June 10th) with very heavy rain, and with the wind going round to the south-west again, then it turned east and died away. I took down the mainsail because *Gipsy* ghosts well under her headsails but is upset by the boom slatting in light winds. I had a talk on the radiotelephone to David Fairhall and his brother, and a long discussion with the engineers about generating electric current. Then I had breakfast and washed up, cleaned the cockpit after Pidgy, and made yet another new tent for him at the after end of the cockpit seat. In the afternoon the wind backed right round through south-east and north-east to north, and we settled down to a broad reach under genoa and staysail. I ricked my back, doing nothing in particular, in the old place where I have had trouble ever since I had a crash in my Gipsy Moth seaplane. It made it very painful indeed to move about, but I thought that with a bit of luck it should be all right, because it is a temperamental ailment.

I generated for the inboard pair of batteries for half an hour until the generator got hot, but it seemed to me to get hot only because the whole motor got hot: I wondered why. I put a pint of Castrol into the gear-box and tried again. There seemed to be much strain from the exhaust, but water came out all right from the cooling system, and I finished another half-hour's charging for the second pair of batteries. In the evening I was just about to have a snooze when the wind backed to the north-west, so I trimmed up on the wind. We were moving well, and it was nice to be on the move again. I couldn't get a sun sight at noon that day because there was no sun, but I managed to get one with the evening sun, and it confirmed my DR position. I found that we had made good a total of 963 miles towards New York.

A terrific disaster (from a yachting point of view) struck during the night. I woke up at five-thirty and rolled an eye over to the 'tell-tale' compass and found that Gipsy Moth was heading north. I thought, oh Lord, the wind has gone round; I must get up quickly and change the sails. But the next thing I knew was waking up at eight o'clock to find that we were heading east. So for an hour or two I had been travelling in the wrong direction. This was terrible—it really breaks the heart of a poor yachtsman. I went out on deck and put her round into the right direction, setting the big genoa, staysail and working jib, and was soon travelling towards New York again with a Force 2 wind.

I was very tired that morning, and as I looked up at the rigging I thought suddenly that yachting is getting fantastic. It seemed mad not to have a rig like Blondie Hasler in his single-sailed junk-rigged Jester. I counted up to thirty different sheets, guys, and tiller lines, and it gave me a nightmare to think of them all. A spider would have a job to find his way around my cockpit. But it didn't do any good to think like this, for the wind was getting up, and I felt that I ought to set the small spitfire jib.

But in the middle of doing so I changed my mind, and said to myself, 'I'll stick to the old working jib'. So I hoisted that up again, thinking while I did so that either I was mad or that my judgement must be terrible, or something. Of course, the truth was simply that I was very tired. And there came a gust soon afterwards which made me wish that I had the spitfire up after all.

I was kept so busy that morning that I couldn't do anything about breakfast until nearly two p.m., when I had my only cooked meal of that day. It was a very good one of fried potatoes, onions in butter, with herring roes, which all went very well together. Breakfast—or lunch, or whatever it was—made me feel better, and I was particularly grateful that my back was better. In the afternoon I had more work to do on deck, and found it very wet. At least one thing you get for free in the Atlantic is barrow-loads of salt water over you for shower baths, and washing the deck.

At night I was too tired to eat again, but managed a few dates and an orange in my bunk. I was interested to find that I could not get hold of the orange peel with my fingers because the nails were worn too far down. I had to turn out again during the night to set the trysail because of the wind. I found that I was working very, very slowly, and was obviously tired out. But I got the work done, and the boat went really well all night, plunging away at 6 knots, and in the right direction. But, my word, it was rough. We simply bounded about all over the place, and time after time I woke up. Once I thought something must have broken because there was a terrific crash, and after that a regular thump every few seconds. I got out and had a good look round, but everything seemed intact. I came to the conclusion that it must have been a can of oil which had broken loose and was rolling from side to side.

I found that I had developed the habit of talking to myself: I think it came through talking first to the pigeon, and then going on talking to myself. Pidgy got very fed up when a terrific sea came down on the cockpit and washed him right out of his little hut, and he wouldn't go back again for a bit. But he cheered up later, and his beak chattered away back when I talked to him.

Tuesday, June 12th, was another busy day. I heated water ready to do two days' washing up after breakfast, but it was not until the middle of the afternoon that I actually managed to do it. I spent much of the morning working on the motor, trying to charge the batteries. The engine varied a lot in speed, running suddenly slowly, suddenly fast, and after forty-eight minutes' charging there was a 'plonk' as my cord locking the propeller shaft broke. Steam blew through the escape holes in the gear-box filler cap, and from the cap astern, from what I assumed to be the clutch. The gear-box was so hot that rain sizzled on it. I concluded that the clutch was engaging periodically although the engine was supposed to be running in neutral. After struggling with the engine I worked hard on Miranda, rigging up a cordage device for double reefing without having to lower her and swing her round to the backstay to do the work. This arrangement was with a light nylon cord from the mast, which hauls up the boom to the reefing eyes: it laces them up, gathering sail as it lifts the boom. It was an arrangement I had needed badly. I also found that a bottle screw which tensions the stay from Miranda's mast top to the end of the spar carrying a 50 lb. lead counterpoise, was missing.

There was a big drop in the barometer, and I began to expect rough weather. Rain fell heavily, and things looked very dirty. The wind gusted up to gale force, and I set my storm sails, but no sooner had I done so than the wind fell off again, leaving me feeling very depressed. I was sick and tired of putting storm sails up, and getting working sails down, and the thought of going all the way round again and setting the old sails was very depressing.

We had about two hours of calm when we could not move at all, then a breeze got up, but still the yacht wouldn't move because of a lumpy swell coming in from the south-west. It was quite a big swell, very rough, and throwing the boat about so much that she could not move, although there was enough wind to make her sail. I tried sailing her downwind in order to get up enough speed before turning off into the waves, but it was no use.

Finally, she got going in the evening. The wind had gone right round the clock, and was trying to go round again. Sometimes I felt that I was going to go mad, trying to trim sails for every shift in wind direction. Anyway, the wind ended up as NNE. and then it backed a little to NW. by N., and we managed to move fairly well under a semi-storm rig. It was a grey and ruthless-looking sea— real Atlantic stuff—and it was very cold. I wore my thick, padded jacket in the cabin to try to keep warm.

I turned in, but woke in the early hours of June 13th to find that we were running quietly enough. But we were not going very fast. What could I do to increase speed? I thought over this for a bit, and then decided to wait until daylight before doing anything, for I badly needed rest. When I got up I eased the sheets, which seemed to put up speed by about half a knot. We had some magnificent sailing later. The sun came out, shining on the great seas, and *Gipsy Moth* crashed through them. It really was wonderful, the way she seemed to like those big seas, and the way she went through them. We were averaging 6½ knots which, in heavy weather and in a boat of *Gipsy's* size, really is something. I was very pleased with her, although I did get a bit apprehensive at times about the tremendous crashes she gave when she bounced over the waves. It was great sailing for me, but not for Pidgy. I saw him catch a sea, and from the look of disgust on his face I decided that he must be a crabby old bachelor.

I noticed that the log had stopped, and I puzzled why. Then I noticed that all the sheet ends had been washed overboard from the deck beside the cockpit. Normally I keep them in the cockpit in seat lockers, but Pidgy fouled everything in the cockpit, so I had left them out. When I hauled them inboard I found that the log line and spinner were tangled with them in hundreds of twists. It was blowing a gale as I got them in, but the sun was shining. A lot of very clear, white, sparkling sea came on board. I downed the working jib and hoisted the spitfire so that I had full storm rig, with spitfire, storm jib, and trysail. I passed extra lashings round the bagged genoa on the cabin top, and checked the trysail and staysail sheets. After doing all this I unravelled the log line and streamed it again. My sextant took a sea sousing when I was trying to get a sight, but I put it under the fresh water tap, and gave it a bath, and hoped that it would be all right.

I had been getting ice reports from John Fairhall, so I plotted icebergs and the ice area on the chart. It seemed good this year. The anchor light gave trouble, and went out three times before I could get it out of the cockpit. It seemed almost a waste of effort to try to carry a light. I turned in with some misgiving, for a change of wind seemed likely.

1 *An R.A.F. photo of* Gipsy Moth *four days out from England*

Francis Chichester in the galley

2 *At the radiotelephone*

Cooking at sea

3 *In the cockpit—note the safety harness that he was meticulous in wearing*

Making sail

4 *Francis and Sheila Chichester*

5 (*Opposite*) Gipsy Moth *under way*

Waving goodbye on setting out

7 *The Navigator*

6 (*Opposite*) Gipsy Moth *under way*

8 *"Pidgy"—a photograph taken by Francis Chichester in mid-Atlantic*

V

Storm

THE thunderous crash of sea which woke me just after three a.m., must have come from a rogue wave, or one at the tail end of a squall, for when I rushed on deck all seemed well enough there. I eased the tiller lines a trifle to sail a shade freer. There was an intermittent moon in a stormy sky, but the sea was moderating, although there were still some visible squalls about.

I got a good transmission to London on twelve megs. after breakfast, and then the wind fell off, and I got out the mainsail in place of the trysail. By noon we were going with all plain sail set—the big genoa, staysail and mainsail. My noon position put us 1,304 miles on the way to New York, with a day's run of 126 miles, of which I reckoned 121 were made good. I managed to get a bit of charge into the batteries. That afternoon, June 15th, was one of mostly shifting winds, and by evening we were more or less becalmed. We were on the move again by ten p.m., but the wind still seemed undecided about what it wanted to do. The pigeon didn't much like things, and I heard him swearing to himself in the dark.

I was woken up, again just after three a.m., by a gust of wind which really laid the boat down. I went up to change the big genoa, but the sky did not look too bad, and I wondered whether I could hold on to it. At five-thirty a.m. I went up to have another look at things. It was still fine, but fortunately I saw what looked like a really dirty squall ahead. Although it seemed a fatuous thing to do at the time, I put up my spitfire jib instead of the big genoa. It meant a change of a 420-square-foot sail for one of 65 square feet: I thought I must be mad—you know, you wonder whether your judgement has gone to blazes—but actually it blew up pretty soon afterwards, and it went on blowing a gale for an hour or two after that. It was interesting to see that in a strong wind the boat went just as well with the spitfire up as with the big genoa. Miranda was

D

thumping badly, so I reefed her, and that made things better still.

I went below to try for a bit more sleep, but after about an hour and a half I most unwillingly crawled from my berth: the going was too rough for sleep. I got the mainsail down and set the trysail. *Gipsy* sailed well like this, but the going was still rough. I felt quite pleased that my judgement about the squall in an otherwise fine sky had been right. I made myself a cup of coffee, and then talked to John Fairhall on the radiotelephone. I had to hold on hard to keep standing as I talked to him. It seemed extraordinary that there was no sign of fog yet: at this time in the Atlantic in 1960 I had been in fog for weeks. But although it had kept clear, I had not seen a ship since the one that circled me at the beginning of the trip.

The sea was getting pretty rough, with *Gipsy Moth* flying into the air every now and again, and landing with tremendous crashes. It is fantastic what these yachts will stand up to, and I felt full of admiration for Jack Tyrrell in County Arklow, who built this boat. There seemed to be some sort of hoodoo on the electrics, for when I was setting the trysail I put my hand on the electric navigation light, and got a shock. That was the way to lose current, and it frightened me to think about, so I disconnected all the lights.

After talking to John Fairhall I had some breakfast, but then found that I could not keep awake, so I dozed off. I awoke to find the yacht getting an awful hammering, and when I saw a dollop of water come through the closed forehatch I decided that I must act. I took down the staysail and lashed Miranda to the backstay. There was peace for a bit, but we were in a full gale from the south-west. I hadn't secured the staysail halliard, and it flew outboard. I was lucky to catch it again. It wrapped itself round shrouds, crosstrees, etc., but at least I had it. *Gipsy Moth* sailed well by herself with trysail and spitfire set. The effect of dropping the staysail was amazing, but it seemed to take all life out of the boat.

I fed Pidgy again, and gave his tabernacle another covering. He let me stroke him, so he must have been feeling pretty fed up. He looked like a sick jackdaw: it must have seemed utter hell to him.

The rest of that day was mostly stormy, and the seas grew very rough—I estimated the waves at about 12 feet. Still, I managed to cook some lunch in the middle of the afternoon, and found the 'cooking belt' that I was wearing a wonderful aid. I seemed unduly fatigued, and kept on wanting to go to sleep. The barometer rose a little, but then started to fall again. The sea was still very rough, but before turning in I thought that we could just about stand the staysail again, and decided to try it anyway.

That was a bad night: everything seemed to go wrong. The anchor light went out three times, waiting each time until I had got it into the cockpit, and once it went out while on a hook in the cabin, without being touched. I spent the best part of two hours trying to reef Miranda, and I was just about to get into my bunk, about two a.m., when the yacht came aback, so it was on with oilies again. Another thing, the ring of my torch parted. I got a bit of sleep after that, but rose at nine o'clock very reluctantly as I felt quite fagged out. I unreefed Miranda, and set a course again. I had a rather poor communication with London, did more sail changing, and then set to work to try to get some charge into the batteries. I managed a bit of charging, but had to stop because the exhaust kept blowing through the pipe.

An extraordinary thing happened while I was having a shave. I looked at the barometer just before I started, and glanced at it again when I had finished. The whole thing took only about ten minutes, but the barometer was reading a millibar lower. I was so surprised that I went and checked from my log to see if I had got the previous reading right; but it was quite right, and it *had* dropped a millibar. So I hustled up on deck as fast as I could, and got the big genoa down, although there was a perfectly clear sky.

Sure enough, as I put up the working jib, it started to blow again, and before I had it properly sheeted in, it was blowing so hard that I had to take it down again. Then I put up the small spitfire in its place, but even that was too much with the storm jib, which I had kept set as a staysail. So I had to take that down, and on the way down it got torn: so I was faced with mending it before I could use it again.

I was bothered about the generator. There are two exhaust pipes from the cylinders and the starboard one seemed to consist only of its asbestos lagging, for the pipe inside had corroded through. I could see the flame inside. I decided to put a piece of tin from a beer can round it, and wrapped it all with some more asbestos from the starter motor. I wished that I could find some way of stepping up the rate of charging: it seemed to waste a tremendous amount of power from the engine, just to get a trickle of charge into the batteries, and I had only enough petrol for about fifteen hours' running left.

That night I changed berths for fear of being thrown across the cabin—I might have broken a box of eggs on the other side. Just as I was in my berth thinking how nice it was for *Gipsy Moth* to steer herself, she tacked and came up aback. So I had to tog up and deal with it. The anchor light went out as usual and, as usual, I had to light it three times before it would stay alight. It was a job, too, in a gale, but I thought that the wind was moderating, and when I got to sleep it was coming from the north-west at no more than Force 6 or 7.

The morning of June 17th found us more or less becalmed again. I used the calm to mend the staysail. My noon position put us 1,533½ miles on the way, and I found that we should miss the iceberg that John Fairhall had been telling me about by 17 miles: not much.

The afternoon brought a breeze again at last, but it wasn't much good because it headed us steadily. It was also raining hard. I felt unsettled, and couldn't get myself into a settled mood; I suppose that was because we had had knock down squalls so often in the evening. But the glass was rising and promised fairer weather. I decided that I would have to tack soon, for with Cape Race to clear I must not get too far north.

The next day, June 18th, brought fog, with visibility down to about 300 yards, and as far as I could make out I was heading straight for that iceberg. I decided that I should have to stay on deck to watch for it. I think I could have got a sextant shot at the moon during the night, but I was too lazy, and too sleepy to get up for it. I began to regret this bitterly, for it would have shown me exactly where I was in relation to the iceberg. But I did manage to get a sun shot of sorts, although there was no horizon, before the fog closed down, and I had to do the best I could with that. But working out this sight gave me what I thought was excessive westing. I was also bothered because my stop-watch had stopped while I was taking the sight, which might have made a difference of plus or minus fifteen seconds. This was not altogether happy for plotting ice data, but I worked out what seemed to be the best course for clearing the icebergs that John and David Fairhall had been telling me about.

I felt very disappointed at the slow speed we had been making, but the pigeon perked up a bit. He sat on the afterdeck, sucking up chopped bread out of his bowl—bread chopped up into little pieces, was one of his favourite dishes. He was a very dainty eater, and would never eat more than three-quarters of anything I gave him.

It rained pretty solidly throughout the day, until about four o'clock in the afternoon, when the rain stopped and I saw a little blue sky. I also saw a trawler, homeward bound to Newfoundland. I got another sun shot in the afternoon, and decided to treat my morning shot as suspect. The wind, which had moderated to about Force 5, began to get up again. With evening the fog cleared, but the sea was rough. The jib sheet parted with a sharp twang, and a great flogging of sail: I was lucky to get the sail down without getting soaked, as I did not have time to put on oily trousers. It was bitterly cold, and my hands were so numb that I had trouble in tying gear.

I had great trouble in getting the yacht sailing again under the the spitfire jib, because of all the shambles of halliards, sheets and things to be sorted out, but at last I managed it. My heart dropped when I got back from the foredeck because I thought that Pidgy was missing: I thought he must have been washed overboard. But in the end I found him back in his locker under the cockpit seat, looking very forlorn, wet, and bedraggled. I gave him one of Stalker Miller's oatcakes—nothing but the best on such an occasion—and he seemed to love it. I took him into the cabin and tried to settle him in a large biscuit tin, but he wouldn't stay, so I returned him to his cubbyhole. I suppose he was used to roosting out of doors, but it was bitingly cold.

With great difficulty I set the trysail. While doing this I was swung round the mast, and the top of my head came into violent contact with the reefing gear of the boom. I was surprised that I wasn't knocked out. But with two sails the boat seemed to go mad, so I hurriedly dropped the staysail and left the trysail on for a bit.

I couldn't set the spitfire because the halliards were still fouled up after the trouble with the jib sheet. I felt that this was my fault because I ought to have turned out and shortened sail some time before the jib sheet parted, but I was working on the motor and I wanted to finish repairs to the exhaust and so held off taking in sail until too late.

That night and the next day brought continuous storm, and I spent about sixteen hours more or less hove to. It was difficult to decide what was the best thing to do. There was a full gale from the south-west, and a very rough sea. There was enough surf to make a surf rider seasick, twisting in every conceivable way. It was no use setting more sail, and I just had to grin and bear it. I had a job to keep warm, and I was wearing long, woollen underpants, plus a thick ski sweater, plus Jaeger's padded nylon jacket; all this, with the Aladdin stove in the cabin going full blast day and night. That stove was always much in demand for drying clothes. I had another go at setting the staysail, but it was no good: there was too much wind, and the sea was too rough. I decided to free *Gipsy Moth* from Miranda's control, for I thought that she might go a trifle better without Miranda snatching at the helm. When I had done this I went below to try to cook something to eat, and I just had a vegetable nearly cooked when the old so-and-so went about. Perhaps this was to show me that I couldn't do without Miranda. Anyway, I togged up again, and put Miranda back in charge. The wind had then gone round to the west, but it was still at least Force 8, or perhaps a bit more.

I decided that something drastic must be done, for we were being driven too fast before the gale. I tried to slow up the yacht by backing the trysail and the spitfire jib, which I did by turning the boat round, hauling the sheets in on that side, and then putting her round again so that both sails were aback. But there was too much wind: it knocked the boat down on her side so I lowered the trysail and tried again with just the spitfire, which is only 65 square feet of canvas. It slowed her up a bit, but she was still doing about 3 knots. That was still too fast, but then I had an inspiration. I turned out again and put the helm hard down. With the helm fixed down, and the spitfire aback, she slowed to about a knot and a half, more or less in the right direction.

We took some heavy seas on board, and twice the shock of a
mass of water hitting the yacht put out the cabin lamp. We made
only about 13 miles in the right direction during the sixteen hours
we were hove to, and although we did a bit better after that we
had another twenty-four hours of gale and didn't do too well. I
got some sun sights on June 19th, though it was very difficult to
get an accurate sextant shot in rough seas. I reckoned that the gale
had lost me two days. Pidgy took it badly, and I got more and more
worried about him. He looked wet and cold, and had scabs round
his eyes. Finally, I couldn't bear to see him looking so miserable,
so I made him a dovecote out of a cardboard box, wrapped him in
some old pyjamas, and put him into it. He just lay there for a while,
but after a time he stood up. I tried him with a biscuit, and he
began eating it. This cheered me up immensely, for I had feared
that he was about to hand in his chips. I felt that it called for a
celebration—a strong lime, with a dash of Squire's gin. (I am not
sure if I have got these the right way round!)

During the night of June 20th–21st the storm blew itself out,
and I came on deck to find the yacht becalmed upon a sunless sea.
I looked round with a feeling of despair at the amount of work to
be done in repairing the damage of the storm. Miranda had
suffered badly; the gooseneck of her gaff had sheared off, and both
the stays to her 50 lb. lead counterpoise weight had carried away.
First, I tackled the gooseneck of the gaff, and it was a difficult and
tricky job, because I couldn't get at a lot of it without acrobatic
efforts hanging over the Atlantic; and the Atlantic was on the
jump after the storm. But I managed to improvise and fit a new
gooseneck. I used a deck screw-eye, which I had inherited with
the old *Gipsy Moth* when I bought her in 1954; with a vice and a
file, it fitted. Then I fitted shackles and lanyards to replace the
stays of Miranda's counterpoise. Another bottle-screw in the stay
to Miranda's boom had shaken itself into the ocean, and I replaced
that with a lanyard, too. I was still worried about the 50-lb. weight,
which I thought most insecure, so I rigged a patent home-made
gadget to strengthen it. I also rigged a line to the outboard end of
the gaff for handling it from inboard: I had found it impossible
to pull in by hand in a wind, and it had a really fierce kick.

As I worked, the feeling of despair with which I'd started slowly left me; if one plods on eternally at a job until it comes out right the desperation disappears.

It looked like becoming a fine morning, so I set the working jib in place of the spitfire. Then I got on with more repairs. All the fastenings on the canvas dodgers had given away, but that was natural enough, for they are made weak to make sure that they will give before anything else does. The rigging all wanted trueing up: it had had a pretty good stretch. But it was wonderful rigging, and it gave me great confidence. So did *Gipsy Moth*—it is a great thing in a storm to have a boat and gear that you feel that you can rely on. One tends to forget the tremendous weight of the seas that come on board; by the noise and crash that some of them make, they must weigh a lot more than a ton. One big sea landed right on top of the cabin during the storm, and I could see the water squirting through under pressure in places where I swear that water has never come through before. And afterwards there was no trace of water's having come through at all, but I actually saw it. That sea must have weighed a ton, at least. It is amazing how the gear stands up to it. Miranda is still rather a new thing, and you can hardly expect her not to have some teething troubles.

The fine morning turned to rain, and with the rain what wind there was shifted a bit, from west to a bit south of west. I calculated that the nearest iceberg was pretty well due west of us, and about 70 miles away. I worked out a course which I reckoned would clear the ice, and started sailing again in a modest way.

VI

The Death of the Pigeon

THIS day, June 21st, brought tragedy: the death of the pigeon.

For some days I had been becoming more and more worried about him, and during the storm I thought that he was going to die. He was half naked—you could see his skin through his feathers—and I felt very unhappy about him. Then I had an inspiration, and remembered what I called 'the Haggis box'. That was a box that Stalky Miller, the artist who draws maps for us, gave me with some shortcake and other things in to take on the voyage. It used to be a box for a coffee percolator, so it had a round hole in it, and made a wonderful dovecote. This was the box that I used to make a nest for Pidgy when I decided that things were just too rough for him in the cockpit, and that he would have to be brought into the cabin. I secured the box to the roof of the cabin, just above the galley. I wrapped him in a bit of my old pyjamas, and after sitting listlessly for a while, he went to sleep, with his tail sticking out of the box. He slept for some time, and awoke with a start at a splash of water on the cabin porthole, and after his sleep he seemed a bit more cheerful.

When I had finished doing repairs, and cleaning up the boat after the storm, I thought that the pigeon's nest ought to be cleaned out too, and I also thought that the pigeon himself ought to have some air and movement. So I put him back in the cockpit, cleaned out his nest, and lined it with some clean sheets of paper which John Anderson had given me originally to prepare notes on for my radiotelephone messages. Pidgy sat on the counter for a bit, and then made to fly off, as he often did, to do a circuit of the boat. I thought that a little flight would be good for him, so I said, 'Yes, go on,' and waved him off. He took off, but stalled into the water a few feet away. He flapped madly to get off again, but couldn't make it, and then flapped towards me, half in and half out of the water, trying to catch us up.

I put the boat round at once and touched him the first time round, but it was very difficult. You could only reach the water where the freeboard is lowest, and then only by sticking your body well out over the side under the lower lifeline. To bring the boat right up to him meant that I couldn't see him from the helm for the last 50 feet or so, because he was hidden by the side of the boat itself. I tried to scoop him out with the gash (slop) bucket on the end of the boathook, but he thought that I was attacking him, and tried to evade the bucket. Time after time I came up to him, and several times I had him in the bucket, but he was washed out as I drew it towards me. It was heartrending to see his pathetic efforts to reach the bucket, only to shy away when I got the bucket near him. I threw over an old piece of sail to try to give him a sort of lifebelt, but I think it must have sunk.

I spent some forty minutes trying to come up to him, and I put about fifteen times. I dared not stop to lower the sails, or to hunt for anything to throw out as a marker, because I needed to watch his tiny head incessantly so as not to lose sight of him in the sea. Finally, at the fifteenth try, I got him in the bucket, and instead of being washed out, he got ducked and stayed in. This time he was inert when I pulled the bucket towards me, and I managed to grab him with my hand, nearly going overboard myself: I had no time to fix a safety belt or such-like. I wrapped him in hot cloths, warmed from some boiling water I had in the Thermos, and applied artificial respiration for about another forty minutes. I reckoned that I was doing it all right, too, because you could see the air coming out of his mouth when I pressed on the right place. After that I filled a hot water bottle, and wrapped him with it in paper, but he was a goner. I felt very sad indeed, though I think that his time was up. His poor, emaciated, sick-looking body had only a few feathers left. I think he had been very sick, and that his number was up. But that did not stop me from feeling very depressed, and I was especially sad because after I had made the dovecote for him, and put him in the cabin, he seemed to have been perking up a little. And all the time that I was trying to rescue him he must have thought that I was attacking him, for if he had trusted me I could have got him back on board nearly at once.

After Pidgy's death I just had to get on with things, so I did some more housework. I filled the petrol tank for charging the batteries, and I filled the Aladdin stove, and also the paraffin bottles that I used for keeping it supplied, because it was easier to pour into the filler from a bottle. I swept the carpet, and tidied up the cabin. I suppose I was working slowly, but I was surprised to find how long each job took, and it was evening before I was through. A breeze arrived after I had some supper, and I hoisted the mainsail and hardened up the sheets. Then it began to rain, but the sea had gone down, and it was nearly calm. We were doing about $3\frac{1}{4}$ knots when I went to bed.

It was rather thrilling at daybreak next morning, June 22nd, to go on deck and to find that we were ghosting along through a thin fog, and a nearly calm sea. I was still feeling fagged and below par, and I felt a little sad when I took my noon sight and found that the sun had started declining southwards: midsummer was over.

I was now well into the Grand Banks, and I reckoned that I passed right over one of the icebergs that John and David Fairhall had been telling me about: it must have melted, or drifted away somewhere else. I decided that my best course was to make some 50 miles south-east of Sable Island. I was allowing for 10 miles setting in the current, but I found that it had been setting me back about 15 miles a day: I concluded that there was an extra strong easterly set in the current because of the long south-westerly gales. We should be in a neutral south-going current soon, from meeting the Labrador current off the Newfoundland coast. I was a bit bothered about these currents because I seemed to be some 52 miles south-east by south of my position as estimated by dead reckoning over three days, which seemed a big error, and I puzzled over the reason or reasons. A finger of the Labrador current could have done it easily, and the water was certainly icy, coming straight down from the Labrador coast. Again, my sights may have been in error three days earlier, but I felt not with errors of as much as 50 miles. But it certainly had been difficult to hold the sextant in a gale, and to decide in the turbulent sea what was a true horizon and not just the back of a distant wave. Furthermore, my dead reckoning was bound to be rough, because of the time I spent below sleeping, etc. On the whole I felt that we had drifted faster south by east than I had logged during the night we had spent with only the spitfire set aback. And one knows that the current at any given point of time is unpredictable. All we do know about the current is that over a period of years it averages so much at this spot in June. I decided to stick to my noon position as logged.

I picked up Radio Gander and heard a weather forecast from them. That night I had a good contact with London, and arranged to call every day at 0900 GMT and 2130 GMT. New York would listen in so that as I got nearer the end of the passage, instructions about meeting me could be given. I felt a new man when I turned in that night: I had had a pounding, and life seemed rotten, but we had sailed 69½ miles since noon.

I felt that I should have to put the skates on to overcome the way in which the storm had mucked me up, but *Gipsy* was going really well over the Grand Banks. There was a curious incident during the night. I woke suddenly in the dark and went on deck. It was foggy as well as dark, and I saw a large steamer looming right across my bows. I put my helm hard down to come up into the wind to pass ahead of her, but she seemed to be moving in the same direction, so I turned downwind. Then it seemed that I would hit her amidships, so I turned back upwind, so that I could swim along with her if she was moving. She foghorned then, and I realized that she was a fishing steamer, and not moving at all. So I cleared her all right. Why did I wake up? Some instinct must have wakened me, like the instinct that warns an animal of danger. Perhaps after many days alone this instinct in man is sharpened.

My hands were so cold that I found it difficult to hold a pen, so I had a *petit déjeuner* of hot grog and a biscuit. I heard a blast from another fishing boat astern, and soon afterwards crossed the bows of a trawler 100 yards away. I was below and they hooted, which brought me on deck, but I did not need to alter course. I had the big genoa boomed out with the working jib on the other side and the mainsail set. *Gipsy Moth* was doing around 6 knots. I felt much improved by having a big wash and a shave. Fog was more or less continuous all day, with visibility varying from about three-quarters of a mile to a quarter of a mile. I managed to get two observations of the sun with the bubble sextant, and the shots all tallied amazingly: I think this must have been a pure fluke, because it is impossible to keep bubble and sun together at sea. Nevertheless, the plotted result agreed with a late sun shot with the ordinary sextant to within eight minutes of arc: I would say that ten minutes' accuracy was as good as one could hope for.

It was a gentle night, with a light fog, and a smooth sea, and we had some wonderful sailing—the kind a sailor always dreams of. After the Atlantic, which seems such a ruthless, hard, kind of ocean, the Banks were like coming home. Morning saw the wind a few degrees forward of the beam and I had the working jib, on a pole out to windward, drawing well. The sea was as smooth as the Solent, and the mysterious Grand Banks were covered with calm gliding water which gurgled and rumbled along the hull. I was then about 78 miles from the longitude of Cape Spear, and about 1,067 miles from New York.

I had a good lunch, with garlic and Danish Blue cheese, preceded by a glass of Mackeson. While I was in the middle of lunch there was a loud bang, and I found that the grommet at the clew of the working jib, holding it to the spinnaker pole, had parted. No harm was done, however, and the trouble was soon remedied. And I had no need to reset the jib, as the wind freshened and the genoa was enough. *Gipsy Moth* was doing 6½ knots.

In the afternoon I got a good sun shot which suggested that we had been given a lift of some 13 miles by the Labrador current. That night we crossed the longitude of Cape Spear, and I felt the real romance of the passage stealing in at last. It seemed to take twenty-four days to shed the materialism of ordinary living.

In the small hours of Monday, June 25th, I got up thinking that we were becalmed, but I found the yacht still moving. A Mother Carey's chick was struggling on the main boom; evidently it had flown into the mainsail. I gathered it into the palm of my hand and presently deposited it on some nylon sail tie stops which were heaped in a corner of the cockpit. It was a quaint little bird, with feet rather like a bat's, with three toes, webbed with a membrane. It had a very curved beak, like a toy parrot's, and a white band across its back where the tail starts. It stirred me to the heart, and after sitting still in the cockpit for a bit, it recovered itself and flew away.

I hated the banging and slatting of the calm, but I left the mainsail up because we kept ghosting along: we did 5 miles in three hours, not record-breaking, but better than nothing. Around nine a.m. I had some coffee in the saloon and made up a second pair of sheets for the jib. That day I could hear the mainland broadcasting promises of very little wind, but I was well offshore and I hoped to find a better wind where I was. But the gentle wind was jolly nice—one could have one's stout and Danish Blue in the cockpit. It meant a lot of work, though, changing sails all day and trying to take advantage of any zephyr that came along. I saw a fine school of porpoise, some of them leaping 10 feet out of the water: I supposed that they were playing. A fishing boat, number 15, came up to me during the afternoon. It was rather amusing the way it went ahead of me, and then turned off in a direction which I made out to be Boston. It was rather as if they thought that I was on the wrong track and they were showing me the right way to go. I still had 948 miles to go to make New York, and only six days to do it in if I was to get there in the thirty days I had set myself. Only a miracle could let me do it, but I felt, 'Never mind; that is the way life goes, and it is great fun.'

We came on the wind again, so I handed the genoa and set the working jib with the staysail, but after a bit the wind freed a bit. It was dropping calm, anyway, so I let the sails stay as they were. The night brought drizzle and more fog, but it stayed calm, and in the light breeze it was clear that the cutter rig was what suited the yacht best. I was glad that I had left the jib and the staysail as they were though it had seemed quite wrong at the time.

I put my clock back four hours because I began to feel like a delinquent getting up at ten in the morning—really, six a.m.—and having lunch at five-thirty in the evening.

I managed to get some more charge into the batteries, but when I tested a cell—the one I always tested—the reading had not gone up at all, although the other cells had gone up to 1·140.

I couldn't explain this. There seemed a lot of witch-doctory about those batteries. Calls from London came through very strongly, although the batteries were so low, and London could hear me well.

My noon position next day, June 26th, showed that we had made good 108 miles since yesterday, which left me 840 more to reach New York. The wind fell off, but I set my ghoster and we still went along at between 2 and 3 knots. In the evening we seemed totally becalmed, and in desperation I decided to turn in and go to sleep. I awoke just before three a.m. to a real shemozzle: instead of the wind coming in a nice little zephyr from the south, it was coming in a really hearty breeze from NNW. I had only one sheet on the ghoster, which I had to get in before doing anything else. It was all over the foredeck and I trod on it all the time, slipping at every step. I had my torch, but, oh, for a light I could see by without having to hold it with my chin! I tidied things up on the foredeck and then I had to tackle the mainsail. I had left it loose ready for the zephyr I had been expecting, and in the wind that came it was flapping madly. In trying to get it up it jammed on the lower shrouds, and I had to come up on the wind before I could free it. However, at last I managed to get it up properly.

To add to those troubles I wasn't feeling too good because I had eaten a rather indigestible supper. I couldn't bear to waste the tomatoes, which were rather past their freshness, but had survived the trip, so I had fried them up and eaten them, but the result was not too good.

Such little things apart, everything was fine. Gone was the calm with its frustrating hard work of trying to humour and coax *Gipsy Moth* into some movement. We now had a very pleasant reaching breeze, and *Gipsy Moth* was slipping along at nearly 7 knots. My course took me about 35 miles south of Sable Island, but it remained well out of sight. The temperature was 52 degrees, and I supposed that meant that I was in an off-shoot of the Gulf Stream, but with the north in the wind, the weather seemed very cold. During the morning a Russian fishing vessel overtook me; maybe she thought that Miranda was some secret weapon! She tooted, which brought me up on deck. She was apparently off to New York. The sun was very hazy indeed through the mist, but I got some sun shots and worked out a position. *Gipsy Moth* was beginning to go really fast, but she was throwing her weight about and roaring as she did so. I took in the staysail and rolled two reefs in the main. The yacht's speed stayed the same, but she went about things more quietly. Miranda gave a bit of trouble, and seemed unable to hold the course. I oiled the rudder stock and decided to give it some more oil daily. I had a good talk to John Fairhall and the BBC, but there seemed something wrong with my starboard aerial; it seemed to have no power in it.

VII

In the Gulf Stream

I TURNED in early that night, June 27th, being pretty sure that I would be called out soon. I was right, for the wind backed somewhat and increased, and just before midnight I had to reef the mainsail, and take in the staysail. We had a mad ride, reaching into the dark, with apparently acres of white water from the bows, and waves sliding past fast. I think we were doing 10 knots—faster than at any other time of the voyage. The sea was moderate, except for occasional combers which tried to roll the boat over, or slewed her stern or bows round. The mast and sails and gear could have taken the strain, I thought, though perhaps not the sails, so to be on the safe side I reefed. I feared for Miranda, who was the weak link. It was a magnificent sail, and tremendously exhilarating. After watching and enjoying things for a bit, I turned in again, and awoke about six a.m. to find the sun streaming into the cabin out of a clear sky. It was marvellous after that rather rocky night, what I call a real Bermudan day. There was a pale blue sky, with a dark blue sea, and some dark yellow pieces of seaweed floating past now and then. Everything was lovely, and there was still quite a breeze blowing. It was not exactly the wind I wanted, for it was mainly from the west, and my best course could be only sw. by s., which was 30–35 degrees off the course which I wanted for New York. I kept hoping that the wind would back into the sw., so that I could change tack and lie closer to the way I wanted to go. I knew that Sheila was due to fly to New York in a day or two and I wanted to be there to meet her, though I didn't expect that I should quite be able to make it.

But the wind stayed westerly and more or less dead on the nose, so I hardened up everything and *Gipsy* drove hard on the wind, still moving at between 6 and 7 knots. I didn't want to get too deep into the Gulf Stream, so I hoped more than ever that the wind

E

would soon back to the sw. On inspecting the foredeck I found to my horror that the jib halliard was over the lee crosstrees. I gave full marks to Sparlight who made the mast and to John Illingworth who designed the rigging for the way in which everything had stood the strain if the halliard had been like that during our rough ride in the night.

I tested the radio batteries and they didn't seem to have any charge in them at all, although they were still prepared to work. I managed to charge them for an hour and twenty-five minutes, and I suppose the engine put some charge in them, but I could not see any difference in the readings.

My noon position put me 42° 15′ N., 61° 47′ W., which made my distance to the Nantucket Light Vessel 360 miles, with another 198 miles to get from there to New York, 558 miles in all. It was such a lovely day that after a glass of Mackeson and some cheese and garlic in the cockpit, I went to sleep where I sat. When I woke up I made a private note for myself that I must prepare to lay off garlic soon because New York was getting so near.

A few minutes before six that evening I did another plot of my position and found that we were 30 miles nearer to New York than we had been at noon, which brought down the distance to 528 miles. I had a good transmission to John Fairhall in London that evening, and at his request transmitted on four megacycles for five minutes to the United States; I found it rather uncanny, not knowing if I had been heard or not. Two west-going steamers overtook us. *Gipsy Moth* was still going well, though when I was down below in the cabin I had a curious feeling, as if she were stalled and stationary. I decided that this was perhaps due to the effect of the particular wave formation round her hull at that moment. When I turned in that night there was a clear sky with bright stars, and the wind seemed to be falling off a bit.

The next day, June 29th, brought rather poor sailing, but it was a wonderful day. I sorted out my new swimming trunks, and they were the only thing I wore all day. I had a sluice down in the cockpit in Gulf Stream water—the temperature of the water was 64 degrees. I felt very sorry for people in London.

It really was absolutely superb out there, although I feared that we were very much in the Gulf Stream. There was hardly a cloud in the sky, and I was able to dry out all my gear, and to get on with doing my housework in the best of conditions. Before I left England I had had some bread baked for me by a vegetarian restaurant called the Vega, and I dug out a loaf, which I found in almost perfect condition. I had some nice cherry jam with it, and beautifully fresh butter: it had all kept admirably. I had a look round at my stores, and I thought that if I was to use them up I should probably have to take a turn round Cape Horn. I had so many things that Sheila had laid in for me that I could not possibly eat through them all. It seemed a rather sad predicament.

For six hours or so we were more or less becalmed, although *Gipsy Moth* still seemed to manage somehow to ghost through the water. I had another wash in the cockpit, which cheered me up a bit because the water seemed much colder, and I thought that we might be edging a bit out of the Gulf Stream. The Gulf Stream is marvellously warm, but there was one thing against it—it was setting me back 7 or 8 miles towards Europe every day. My noon position that day showed that I had made 95 miles from noon on the day before. I felt that I was damned lucky to have done this through the hours of calm we had had.

Throughout the afternoon I trimmed sails and made little changes here and there to try to get a bit more speed out of the yacht. I touched up the jib and hardened the sheet a very little, and I also hardened in the main a very little. The water temperature in the afternoon was again 64 degrees. I got some more sun shots and went over the figures. According to my latest sun shot it appeared to me that we had had a Gulf Stream drift of $7\frac{1}{2}$ miles ENE., since six-thirty that morning, which meant about 0·85 knot against us all the time. I felt that I *must* get out of it. I had another good transmission to London, and tried again to woo New York Radio. I tried for seven minutes, but got no reply, and since I had no battery juice to spare I switched off. Around seven o'clock that evening I was puzzled, and rather bothered to meet some sea coming in from the west, which slowed down the boat. I freed the sheets and headed off the wind to try to cope with it. I knew that we were climbing up the continental shelf, so to speak, but we were not over any special canyon, and I couldn't make out what was causing the sea. At last it dawned on me—of course, it was the usual Gulf Stream pobble. I kept on taking the temperature of the water, and at nine-fifteen found that it was down to 62 degrees. This did not seem to mean much.

At midnight it was so calm that the sails were not even slatting, and I could see the planet Jupiter reflected in the surface of the sea. All the stars were visible, though none was particularly bright. To my astonishment at one a.m. the speedometer read 3·5 knots. I couldn't believe my eyes, but on looking over the side I could see that we were in fact ghosting through the water. I thought the speedometer must be off colour, for I reckoned that our speed was about 1¼ knots; that would have been quite marvellous enough in scarcely any wind at all. I thought of easing the sheets and heading a bit more off what wind there was, but I decided that it would be a shame to disturb a trim which was achieving such results. I wanted to keep an eye on the speedometer on the counter, but I couldn't read it very well from the cockpit because there were some drops of water on the glass face, and these reflected back the light from my torch. So I got out a 10-foot bamboo, and with a bit of cloth on the end made it into a wiper for wiping the face of the speedometer; it worked well. Still intrigued by the speedometer, I turned out again at two o'clock to have another look at it, and to see if I could check the results. I did manage to work out our position, and I found that *Gipsy Moth* had in fact done 2⅛ nautical miles in the hour. She was going much faster then, and audibly sailing. The speedometer then read 5¼ knots. The mean of the two readings at the beginning and end of the hour gave 4½ knots, but *Gipsy* had actually done 2⅛ nautical miles over the hour. I decided to make a graph for the instrument to correct its readings at these lower speeds.

I came to the conclusion that *Gipsy*'s ghosting ability was improved by the fact that I was sailing alone, and had no crew. If a boat has once started moving she will go on ghosting along in a fantastic way, provided that you keep very still. If you fill the boat up with a crew and they all go stamping all over the place they will stop it. I decided to help *Gipsy* by going to sleep.

At seven o'clock that morning, June 30th, the temperature of the water was down to 60 degrees. The barometer had fallen a very little, but it was another fine and sunny summer's day. There was a zephyr coming from the sw., which was a bit more what I wanted, although it wasn't very much. I lifted the mainsail on the mast to take up whatever slack there might have been, and played on the sheets, but this brought no apparent change in speed. I got a sun shot just after eight a.m. and found that we had lost another 6 miles to the Gulf Stream. I found that I was just 81 miles ESE. from my position during the 1960 race. Then, it had taken me four and a half days to make New York; I hoped that it wouldn't take so long this time. I heard a radio broadcast from New York, which promised an east wind, and I decided to set the big genoa to be ready for it if it came, but I had breakfast first, for I thought that there might very probably be no need for the big sail, anyway. After breakfast I decided that it might be useful, so I did set it. The speedometer seemed to have gone off the air— I hoped not from taking umbrage after my remarks about it! It was very hot working in only my Jantzen swimming trunks, with my safety belt, and I burned my back a bit in the sun. A little wind did get up, but it was still from the sw. I boomed out the working jib to its full length to port and had nearly full sail set—1,111 square feet.

At noon I found that I had still 429 miles to go to New York. We passed through a narrow band of white froth and yellow sea-weed, 25 yards wide, and stretching as far as I could see both ways. The sea seemed to be a bit smoother on the entry side.

I charged the batteries for an hour and thirty-six minutes, and what a din the engine made! I felt that I still had to go on playing with the sails, but could get nothing in the way of an improvement in speed. I took down the poled-out jib because the wind seemed to be coming from a bit too much ahead, and I tried playing the main and genoa sheets, but got nothing out of it all. With evening, the barometer began dropping fairly fast, so I took in the big genoa. I had a bit of trouble with the jib which I set in its place, because a shackle got caught behind the foretopmast stay, causing a twist in the tack of the sail, so I slackened away the halliard and unfastened and re-fastened the shackle. There was still a lovely balmy air, but I thought that I could see what looked like rain squalls ahead. I decided to put back the clock to Eastern Standard Time of the USA: that made it five hours less than British Summer Time.

The rest of that night I spent trying to catch the wind, changing and resetting sails time and time again. It was a long night, because I had put the clocks back. A wet fog came up and I could see that I was going to get wet in the cockpit, so I changed from pyjamas into my Jantzen swimming trunks. Some blocks were hitting the spinnaker pole and making an irritating noise, so I had to damp them down. During the early morning *Gipsy's* speed seemed to drop for a bit, and I couldn't make out why. The boom had been banging for a time, and she never likes that, but I had stopped it. I think she must have been becalmed, or nearly so, for a time. I tried to sleep, but through the cabin porthole I saw lightning away to the north, so I got up and retrimmed the sails. It was still misty, but clear overhead, and *Gipsy Moth* was going better. I hardened up all the sheets, but the wind swung round as I was doing so. I tried to put her on the starboard tack, but we ended up heading SSE., in a calm. I eased the sheets again, and gradually brought her back to a better course.

Dawn brought a greenish sea, and again I took the temperature of the water. It was 54 degrees, which I took to be the influence of the Labrador current. It was still foggy, and I began hearing steamers round me. I was not too comfortable about them, and I got ready to start the motor in case I needed it to get out of the way in a hurry. I was not going to use the motor unless I was driven to it of course, but it seemed better to make sure that everything was ready.

This morning, July 1st, saw me thirty days out from Plymouth, but I was still 340 miles short of New York. I tried the other tack again to see if I could make more progress, but it was dropping calm. Tacking seemed a waste of time, but there we were, and I couldn't bear to see the boat heading away from the objective. I tacked again and again; it seemed pretty hopeless, but we did succeed in making a rustle through the water. It was rather uncanny to be moving through an oily, smooth surface, and to see swells moving under it before the wind had had time to wrinkle it. I wanted to try to get some more charge into the radio batteries. but I did not like to run the motor with steamers hooting in several quarters at once in pretty thick fog, because the noise of the motor made it difficult to hear the steamers. I must then have been in or near the main steamer channel of the Eastern Seaboard, where it rounds George's Bank. I laid a course which would take me north of George's Shoal, but I knew that if we wavered about we might hit the middle of it. I wrote in my log, '*Wind, oh wind, blow fair for little Gipsy Moth.*'

At lunchtime we were still more or less becalmed, but I was entertained by a large pod of whales—grampuses, I think—which appeared to be coming straight for *Gipsy Moth*. I thought that they might get annoyed if they hit us, so when one lot were about 10 yards away, I blew my foghorn, which I had handy for steamers. They dived under the boat, and came up about 50 yards on the other side. It was an uncanny business: there were two schools of them, coming from different directions, and as soon as they met there was a tremendous swirling of water, and they all disappeared. They seemed to be playing. They were so close to each other that I could not decide if each had two dorsal fins, or whether one was following the other so closely as to make it seem like that. There were steamers hooting everywhere. One can become over-sensitized to noise, and I think I was then, a bit. I heard what I took to be a diaphone to the north, and it turned out to be my rudder stock, moaning.

The wind went to and fro, to and fro, swinging round from NE., through W., to SE. In the late afternoon we began to move again, and since there seemed to be fewer steamers about, I thought that I would charge the batteries. I charged for a time, and when I switched off I had a shock: I heard the sound of running water. I looked in the bilge, and saw it half full of water, which I measured and found to be 17 inches deep. Suddenly seeing water like that in a boat is a shock: where was it coming from? How big was the hole? I located the trouble at the joint of the pipe with the silencer cooling jacket—the pipe was fractured and water, pumped up by the engine for the cooling system, had been coming through. Having located the trouble, I could not remember where the sea cock was for turning off the water in that pipe. Finally, I did remember that it was underneath the seawater filter for the engine. The pipe was too hot to touch, so I just put a piece of tape round it, and then wound cord round that. Turning off the sea-cock was also a problem, because of the hot engine parts round it, but in the end I managed to turn it off without getting burned—not much burned, anyway. That secured things for the moment, and then I set about pumping to empty the bilges.

I knew that I would have to think out what I could do to make a better repair of the burst pipe before long, but I was tired after pumping, and although it was only about six-thirty in the evening, I decided to try to get some sleep. I awoke about eight-thirty to find that the wind had veered to the NE. That made it rather awkward to lay the course I wanted without booming out my twin jibs, but I was against doing this at night after having had such fickle winds all day, so I trimmed up as best I could and went back to my bunk.

I was up again at midnight, and again at two a.m., both times to trim the sails. There was a clear sky, with all the stars showing. I turned in again, but at half past four I was woken up, or thought I was, by a loud crack. I dressed and went on deck, but could find nothing wrong there, and nothing to change. I hardened the main sheet a little, but then decided that it had been better as it was before, so put it back again. I thought that the course was perhaps a little too high, but she slowed down if paid off, so I left her.

After turning in again at five-thirty a.m., I slept until eight o'clock. I must have slept particularly well, for I awoke with a sense of heavenly luxury, and feeling a new man compared with yesterday. My dumps then were chiefly through fatigue. I did my usual chores, checked the jib sheets, and hardened the main sheet, but alas, the wind was dying down. I got a sun sight, but on working it out I came to the conclusion that it was not dependable, and decided to try again after breakfast. But there were other things to do, too. I had to try to get some charge into the batteries, and I had to have a go at the beastly dirty engine pipe where it had sprung a leak. The temporary repair seemed to be holding, so I decided to put off tackling the pipe until after I had got my noon sight. I took the temperature of the water again, and it was 52 degrees, so I was glad to think that we were in the Labrador Corridor, and being helped along a bit. I had a shave, and the wind backed while I was shaving, so I had to go back on deck and retrim the sails. A fishing schooner seemed to be overhauling me, but he crossed astern instead; he was headed for Nantucket Island, I would say.

My noon position put me 224 miles from New York, and I reckoned that we had sailed about 110 miles in the past twenty-four hours, and made good about 114, the extra 4 miles being a bonus from the Labrador current.

It was really time for lunch, but the pipe job was on my conscience, and so I got down to it—literally very much down, for I had to get my head right into the bilge to get at the pipe. It was a horrible job, and it took me until about half past three in the afternoon. Having missed lunch, I gave myself a Mackeson, and reckoned that I deserved it. The repairs seemed satisfactory, so I started the motor to charge the batteries. The exhaust flame was beginning to show through again where I had done my earlier repairs to the exhaust pipe, but the water pipe repair seemed to be okay. I gave the batteries a bit of charge, but I didn't run the engine long for I didn't want to risk things.

The wind was steadily heading us, but *Gipsy Moth* kept going at about 4 knots. It was a perfect sunny day, and it was rather like sailing on a slightly wrinkled mill-pond. During the afternoon what I took to be the Texas Tower became visible in the NW. I soon identified it as the Texas Tower, and it stayed in sight all evening. This Texas Tower is one of those 'early warning' towers, and a mate of the one that was sunk 90 miles SE. of New York in a storm in 1960. There seemed to be a mirage all round, and the top of the tower showed like a natural dome on long mirage-stilted legs. I watched the top half of the sun set through my X7 binoculars. It was a fascinating and wonderful sight, with an unusual reflection, which caused the mirage. The sinking sun took all sorts of shapes. At one moment it looked like a heap of dumped molten metal of irregular shape, then it appeared like a priest's flat hat, and finally like a thick cake tin, with upright edges. A green wisp followed its disappearance. The sky was totally clear of cloud, with a purplish rim of haze all round the horizon, rather like heather mixture. It appeared to be dead calm, but *Gipsy Moth* ghosted along nicely. She was doing $4\frac{2}{3}$ knots, although it seemed incredible.

I had a good talk to London, and afterwards at last contacted

New York Radio. They told me that Sheila had arrived safely, and I arranged to make another call next day.

I was glad of the help from the Labrador current, although it was not all one way because it made everything much colder. I had to have the stove in the cabin on again, and I could no longer afford to take my pyjamas off when I went on deck at night to avoid getting wet. I thought again about those grampuses I had seen yesterday, and I suddenly remembered that for the first time on the voyage I had my fishing line out. (I didn't catch anything.) The same thing had happened in 1960 when I tried to catch a fish on the Grand Banks: I had hardly got the line down when a crowd of whales turned up. But I don't go for the big stuff— not when I am racing!

The early hours of July 3rd saw us headed by the wind again, so I tacked. It wasn't much good, so I tacked again, but it still wasn't any good, and I felt that things were terrible. The trouble was I had got spoilt; I had got used to ghosting at a good speed with a light air, but naturally *Gipsy Moth* couldn't do just what I wanted when she was hard on the wind. Anyway, I couldn't change things, so I stayed on the tack we were on. It was just as well, for a little later the wind suddenly shifted round about 100 degrees, and it would have done us no good if I had been sound asleep while we were on the other tack. I freed the sheets and reset Miranda for a reach. The wind fell off again with daylight, but left us still moving gently to the west. While I was down below looking over the engine I heard an aeroplane overhead. It seemed to say, 'Wake up, this is America'. Around eleven o'clock that morning I saw a rather smart fishing boat—New York seemed to be getting nearer. But the wind kept going all round the clock, demanding endless sail changing. Much sail changing is a weariness to the flesh, but it seemed almost fun that day because of the gorgeous weather. I wore swimming trunks and shoes only, and had a good sea wash in the cockpit. I saw more fishing boats, some with four or five chaps on them.

At lunchtime there was no more bread, for what I still had left had become too mouldy to eat. We spent the rest of that afternoon hard on the wind, and around four o'clock I changed the genoa for the jib. That seemed to send her speed up a bit, and we covered

6·1 miles in the next sixty-five minutes. I had a sort of race on with myself, for I was only 15 miles behind my position for the same time of day on July 20, 1960. I had been pretty well becalmed then, 12 miles SW. of Montauk Point, but I remembered that I had had a very fast sail for nine hours after that. I would have my work cut out to overtake myself on my sail in 1960, and I hoped that the wind would hold. When I talked to David Fairhall in London in the evening he told me the forecast was that the wind would hold.

I couldn't tear myself away from the deck; it was perhaps my last night's sail of the race, and *Gipsy Moth* was going her best. It was almost the same wind and speed of our riotous ride down Long Island on July 20–21, 1960. At seven forty-five that evening I had my first glimpse of land for thirty-two days, when I saw Block Island in the distance. At nine fifty-eight I saw a faint flashing light, which I took to be Montauk Point, although the map advised against it because the Montauk Point light flashes every ten seconds, and this seemed to be flashing every five seconds. If it were not Montauk, it meant that my dead reckoning was slightly out—about $2\frac{1}{2}$ miles—which could have been due to the tide.

At ten thirty-seven the light bore 013 degrees, and seemed to be flashing at eight seconds. I calculated that it was 19·4 nautical miles away. By my earlier reckoning we should have been 22·2 miles from it, but the tide would account for the difference. At eleven twenty-five I picked up a light flashing every five seconds and bearing 032 degrees, and at eleven forty-two a ten-second light. We were doing pretty well, and I reckoned that we had covered 10·2 nautical miles in 104 minutes, but the wind then dropped and headed us. I was fagged out with all the messing about of the wind.

But I couldn't go to sleep because the wind was heading me into the land. So I went about and put *Gipsy* on the other tack, which led right out to sea, towards Bermuda or somewhere. That at least seemed safe enough, so I turned in and went to sleep. I slept soundly for about four hours, and woke with a start to see N. on the 'tell-tale' compass beside my eye. I jumped out into the cockpit in my pyjamas and there was the land right ahead, about 2 miles off. The wind had veered and swung *Gipsy* round in a semi-circle while I slept, and she was charging straight ashore. I had got on deck just in time. Again, why did I wake up when I did? As with the incident of the steamer on the Grand Banks, some instinct seems to have warned me of danger while I slept. Calculating the results of all those night antics I estimated that *Gipsy Moth* had sailed about 19½ miles while I had slept.

We were past the Shinnecock Light, and at six-fifty I reported my position to New York Radio, and asked how to pronounce Shinnecock. I heard the Edith G. Whisky Hotel asking for information about *Gipsy Moth III*.

I boomed out the big genoa, and felt that we were getting on. At eight-fifteen we passed the Moriches Buoy, logging 5¾ knots. But that was the speed through the water, and we were covering ground a bit better than this because of a favourable tide. At ten-fifteen we had 47 miles to go, and I called New York Coast-guard Radio and gave my position. The wind shifted to ESE., and I boomed out the jib as well as the genoa and gybed, but the wind didn't hold, and went round to the SW., so I had to get down the genoa and set the staysail with the working jib, and put *Gipsy* hard on the wind. I was certainly made to work that morning—a list of sails changed and trimmed would make a good PT syllabus. I pushed into the shore and tacked, then tacked again, and I quite forgot about taking a noon sight until twelve-thirty. I worked out my position then, and found that I had still 44 miles to go to reach the Ambrose Light Vessel. I had a point of land to clear, and had some difficulty in clearing it, tacking back and forth, inshore and out again.

In the middle of the afternoon I suddenly saw a great line of poles all wired up and sticking out half a mile from the coast. I found out later that they had big fishing nets suspended from them, presumably to make fishponds. They were not shown on the charts, and I would have charged straight into them if I had not noticed them. It was a bit of luck that I did so, and as it was I had to pinch hard to scrape past without tacking.

I spoke on the radio to John Fairhall in London, and arranged to call again when I got to the Ambrose Light. The batteries were very low, and I felt that I must try to put some charge into them, although it was a damned nuisance. I started the engine for charging, but what with one thing and another I didn't make much of a job of it. First, I connected positive to negative, and I was amazed to see a sudden discharge of 15 amps. I hoped that no great harm was done. Next, the ammeter started charging right off the scale at times. I hunted round, felt the generator, etc., and found that the battery connection was touching other metal as *Gipsy Moth* rocked. In spite of all this, the batteries survived.

At six twenty-eight I passed a buoy that was 12 miles from the Ambrose Light Vessel. The wind freshened, and I had to take in the staysail. This was a nuisance, but it was too fresh to carry it without slowing down. At eight minutes past eight I could see the Ambrose Light Vessel, and the end of my passage. I held my course for a bit, but I could see that I would have to tack to reach the light vessel. At nine o'clock I made my tack, and headed for it. At nine-seven the Ambrose Light Vessel confirmed that *Gipsy Moth III* was crossing the line.

Note: That was just after two a.m. British Summer Time. In spite of the fact that he was in a busy shipway, and had his hands full in navigating Gipsy Moth, *Francis found time to dash below and call up London. He just managed to report that he had 'crossed the line', and then he signed off, saying that he must get back on deck to see to things. The radio and its batteries kept going to the last. J.R.L.A.*

VIII

'A Marvellous Sail'

WELL, I missed my 30-day record: I took 33 days, 15 hours and 7 minutes. So I am left with my ambition to do it in 30 days. But, you know, it does not depress me at all; it was a marvellous sail.

I remember when I started ocean racing I analysed the winning time of RORC races over a number of years for Class III yachts, and I believe the majority of those races were won at an average speed of less than a hundred miles a day. This does not sound fast, but consider the effect of four hours of calm per day, how much faster you must sail during the other twenty hours. Then there is the slowing up by a headwind when, for every 5 miles sailed, you advance only 3 miles towards the destination.

I left with a big feeling of responsibility towards my friends who had put so much faith in my attempt. There was no room for the 1960 romance and sense of adventure, when it was a terrific thrill to arrive both at the starting and finishing line. This time I had to race hard every minute I could. Whenever I knew that a sail would have been changed or retrimmed if I had a full crew, and I did not change that sail because I was exhausted, or for some other reason, it worried me. And one of the hardest things of the voyage was to use sound judgement in deciding what to do. All the time it was weighing up the situation. For instance, the yacht would go faster at this moment if the big genoa were boomed out. Very good; but probably the wind will have backed 100 degrees in four hours, and the time lost in setting and unrigging the big spinnaker pole, during which the sail is doing no work, will produce a net result less than if I jogged along with the original sail setting unchanged. Or this problem might arise just before I was going to sleep, when there was always a strong chance of being awakened by a gust or squall, when handling the 21-foot pole etc. in the dark was a danger to limb in a strong breeze, besides losing time.

I was thrilled when I covered the first 1,000 miles of the route in ten days, but felt I was losing the battle because conditions had been good up to then. Then came the three-day gale. Being able to beat into a Force 8 gale is something that just could not have been done at all by small yachts a few years ago. But now, in waters like the English Channel, it is a wonderful success for the designers of the modern cruiser-racer. In the broad Atlantic, however, with a really rough, turbulent sea, it is hardly possible to make progress, and it certainly is a hell of an existence. I did stipulate that I could see no hope of making the thirty-day passage without the luck to avoid a storm. Even so, I made the loss of time worse than need be; I made a tactical blunder. The NW. tack looked best for New York, and was the textbook leg to take. I took it—my big mistake. It needs a long explanation; briefly, had I worked south through-out the storm I would have made better use of the prevailing wsw. wind during the following week, without being forced up NE. of Newfoundland.

After the storm I only lost about two hours over my attempts to keep the pigeon alive, but I was so upset at my failure, due to relationship between man and creature, that I bungled the whole of that day's sailing. I don't believe I can ever forget the sight of that pigeon in the water, flapping madly, trying to catch up the boat and then during the fifteen circuits and passes I made at it, how it tried to elude my clutch because it treated me as an enemy grabbing at it instead of a friend. However, it was no good getting into a mood of failure, and I pulled up my mental socks and sailed hard from then on.

All down the 1,000 miles of American eastern seaboard, *Gipsy Moth* seemed to go like never before. I suppose, to be matter of fact, I had learned how to handle her with the new rig. It gave me a great thrill. I seemed to know what sails were going to be needed hours ahead, seemed able to trim for much faster sailing, and I got a great sense of achievement from the way she reached out for New York. And this applied to all points of sailing, running, reaching, fetching, and hard on the wind. I could not seem to get her top speed average up above $6\frac{2}{3}$ knots—though I reckon she was doing 10 knots one night, with full sail set, in a Force 6 wind—but her lower speeds all seemed to have increased a lot with the new Illingworth rig.

What a wonderful sail, that thousand miles along America. Sailing such as we never get in the English Channel, it seemed to me, ghosting at $1\frac{1}{4}$ knots one night in a sea so smooth that I could see the planet Jupiter reflected in the sea, or doing 7 knots through a surface like a wrinkled mill-pond. One day I cut out $159\frac{1}{2}$ miles, which I think is good going for a 28-foot-waterline boat. That included the night when we did 10 knots. My log says: 'A mad ride reaching into the dark, with apparently acres of white water from the bows, and waves sliding past. The sea is moderate, except for occasional combers which roll the boat down or slew her bows or stern round.' Part of that day I was hard on the wind. That sums up the thrill of sailing.

IX

Independence Day

FRANCIS CHICHESTER'S own narrative ends with his brief summary in the last chapter of what he regarded as his successes on his voyage, and of his failure to achieve his personal ambition to make the crossing in thirty days. But that is not quite the end of the story. Other people were less concerned with what Francis regarded as his 'failure', and saw his voyage more clearly as the magnificent achievement it was.

After crossing the finishing line by the Ambrose Light Vessel, Francis made his way to the US Quarantine Station at Staten Island, and then started his propeller for the first time in thirty-four days. On the way, he passed the *Queen Elizabeth*, homeward bound. The officer on watch recognized *Gipsy Moth III*, and the great *Queen* acknowledged the little sailing boat's triumph by dipping her colours, and giving her a regal salute of three blasts on her siren. It was a moving gesture.

As he landed at Staten Island, Francis was handed a telegram from President Kennedy, which said:

'I would like to extend my hearty congratulations to you on your successful new record-breaking crossing of the Atlantic. Your skill and gallantry as a sailor are already well known, but this new achievement will certainly cap your career. And we are particularly pleased that you arrived in the United States on July 4th, the great historic day in US history when we celebrate our independence.'

The President's message was but the first of a great shoal of congratulations. H.R.H. the Duke of Edinburgh, whose own yacht, *Bloodhound*, was just then being fitted-out, sent this cable:

'Delighted to see that you have achieved your ambition to beat your own record. All members of the Guild [of Air Pilots and

F

Navigators, of which Chichester is a member] and millions of other admirers send their hearty congratulations on a magnificent achievement. Philip.'

Mr Reginald Bevins, the Postmaster-General, telegraphed to the Editor of the *Guardian*:

'Please convey my congratulations to Mr Chichester. I am delighted to know that the Post Office was able to contribute to the success of the voyage.'

Mr H. G. Mason, Lord Mayor of Plymouth, sent this message:

'Delighted at your success. Plymouth sends hearty congratulations.'

Mr D. P. Furneaux, Managing Director of Marconi Marine, cabled:

'Heartiest congratulations from all at Marconi Marine. Magnificent effort even though not thirty days. Too bad about Pidgy but delighted Kestrel kept so healthy on diminishing diet of volts. Looking forward to your welcome home again.'

One of the messages which gave Francis most pleasure was sent directly to him over *Gipsy Moth*'s radiotelephone by the Post Office people who had been keeping radio watch on him throughout his crossing. This said:

'Heartiest congratulations courageous on splendid trip. We are sorry you were not able to accomplish your hoped thirty days' voyage, but nevertheless it is a magnificent achievement. Well done. With our best wishes for a safe and pleasant voyage home. From Gray, Woolford, and the ETE staff, myself, and all the WTS staff. Graham Wilson.'

Mr Wilson, it may be remembered, was the Assistant Inspector of Wireless Telegraphy whom I went to see in the very early days to discuss whether the radiotelephone experiment was worth trying. The whole radio side of the voyage owed much to him, and to the enthusiastic work of his colleagues.

A particularly moving message came from Sir Geoffrey de Havilland, of the de Havilland aircraft company, after whose original Gipsy Moth Francis's *Gipsy Moth III* was called. 'Friends at Hatfield send warmest congratulations on this latest Atlantic crossing, which revives thoughts of your Tasman adventure and other happy memories,' he cabled. The Royal Yacht

Squadron, the Royal Geographical Society, the Institute of Navigation, the Royal Aeronautical Society, the Royal Ocean Racing Club, the Royal Aero Club and the Guild of Air Pilots and Air Navigators were among those who cabled congratulations. So did much of British industry, including Shell, British Nylon Spinners, John Shaw (wire ropes) and Chloride Batteries, whose products all played a part in bringing *Gipsy* safely to New York.

Although Francis would have preferred to make New York on July 1st, it gave a pleasant touch to the end of his voyage that he should get there on July 4th, during the celebration of Independence Day. The *New York Herald-Tribune* published a photograph of the *Queen Elizabeth* dipping her colours to *Gipsy Moth III*, and wrote of Francis Chichester:

'Under sail, unaccompanied, with no crew but a vagabond, hitch-hiker pigeon (which died) he crossed the Atlantic in thirty-three days, bettering his own forty-day record set in 1960. In a week that saw three new nations gain independence while the United States celebrated the anniversary of its own, this intrepid British adventurer proved anew that independence can belong to men as well as to nations.'

An unofficial reception committee was set up by Mr Laurens Hamilton, a distinguished member of the New York Yacht Club, and a grandson of J. Pierpont Morgan. Mr Hamilton put a splendid 75-foot yacht, *Shadow Isle*, at the disposal of Sheila Chichester and her friends, and took them out to meet Francis on his way into New York Harbour.

New York took Francis to its heart, and gave a great welcome to this one-man British invasion on Independence Day. Alistair Cooke, the *Guardian*'s distinguished New York correspondent, sent a delightful piece about it to the paper. Here it is:

'Independence Day intruder
From Alistair Cooke
New York, July 4th.

'Just to show how one thing can lead to another, how relatively responsible men can put two and two together and get 1776, let me recount as baldly as I can some events of Independence Day.

The whole confusion seems to have set in because a British fleet, squadron, or whatever, was thought to be hovering off Long Island.

'Did it intend to seize West Point, proclaim a monarchy, and revoke the Declaration of Independence? It was known to be in radio contact with England but either could not or would not respond to shore to ship calls from here.

'Most probably the British had been careful to see that they didn't have the proper crystals, or mega-whatnots, to allow communication with this coastline. Well, that started it. The United States Coast Guard got busy. (The Navy can run the Coast Guard only in wartime, and there was no proof yet that that's what this was. In peacetime, the Coast Guard is beholden only to the orders of the Secretary of the Treasury—and let's not go into that, the story is wild enough already.)

'The Coast Guard sent out patrols last night, but no soap. The Coast Guard station at Staten Island had no word of any incoming invasion and said that "that is up to Operations, any-way tomorrow is a holiday". Then they managed to "fix" a suspicious-looking object "becalmed off Nantucket". This was later identified as a cutter with a one-man crew. And that (can you imagine?) is what all the fuss was about. Turned out to be a cheerful-voiced English character name of Chichester. Said he just wanted to sail into New York with no help from anyone but thanks all the same.

'Now, of course, the Coast Guard realized in a flash that its job was to help. But now also the British Embassy and the British Information Services here were manfully getting into the act and before you could say "hold, enough!" they had duty officers manning telephones and stacking up with coffee and sandwiches against the night watch. The helpful calls between Washington, New York, the Third Naval District (they just wanted to be kept informed), and the Coast Guard got so mixed up that at one time the Coast Guard couldn't say what was the direction of the off-shore winds. We offered our services and called a yachting maniac we know who lives in Manchester (Eng.). He said the winds off Long Island were "north to north-east at 10 miles an hour".

We were happy to call up the Coast Guard and set them straight.

'Once the invasion myth was exploded, everyone except the weatherman gave his all to see that this Chichester guy got what was coming to him, namely, a little convoy up the river and genial clearance from Dr Erwin C. Drescher, the chief of the US Quarantine Station here, a happy, benevolent man who took no stock in the invasion story in the first place.

'This morning the Coast Guard was really on the ball. They routed us out of bed to say that "at 0655 hours, the *Gipsy Moth* was 8½ miles west of Shinnecock Inlet, about 76 miles from Ambrose Light". Then at eleven this morning he was 1·4 miles off Moriches Inlet, going at about 3½ knots.

'By now the big question here is why would a man (seems he's in his sixties) want to do such a thing. Happily, your correspondent was able to get an exclusive on that one. A confidential source gave him a tip and set him going through the airplane manifests at Idlewild. BOAC had a record of an incoming lady with an English accent, a rare enough thing around these parts to cause some comment. After going through hotel registers our man tracked her down to a Park Avenue inn.

'From there the trail led to Flushing Yacht Dock. The dockmaster positively remembered "a tall, no-nonsense English lady" going aboard a yacht called the *Shadow Isle*. A quick riffle through "Lloyd's Register of American Yachts" identified a 75-foot cruiser: a call to the marine operator and we had her radio call letters. In no time flat the very voice of Mrs Chichester (for it was none other) was on the horn.

'We cornered her at last tied up (the *Shadow Isle*, of course) at the Quarantine Station on Staten Island. There she said her husband was trying to sail the Atlantic alone the hard way, from east to west, in ten days less than his record time of forty and a half days in 1960. He had had a satisfyingly terrible ordeal then, including a hurricane. Apparently, things had not gone quite so well this time, but it had been uncomfortable enough and he'd enjoyed some spanking Force 8 winds. The yacht seemingly calls for a crew of six, so Chichester is going it alone.

'Anticipating the question which is now ringing around New York harbour (Why? Why? Why would anyone want to do such a thing?") Mrs Chichester said: "Because he likes it." There seems to be no sensible retort to that. Turns out that Mrs Chichester is going to sail the *Gipsy Moth* back, with her 16-year-old son. Some people will never learn.'

To us on the *Guardian*, one of the nicest—and most unexpected—things about the adventure was the way in which schoolchildren all over the country followed it. Letters from them poured into the office, wishing him luck ('I hope you don't hit a boat when going into New York harbour') and sympathizing with him on the death of the pigeon. Two days after the end of the voyage, a London schoolmaster sent us an account of how his class had followed the adventure. He wrote:

'When Francis Chichester set off on June 1st, I decided that my class of London nine-year-olds should know all about it. The first couple of days out they listened politely enough as I read from his log, but by then, as he had neither sunk nor got halfway, their interest began to wane. A pity, I thought. If they would only latch on, there would be food for their starved imaginations for a month or more. But the idea of solitude meant nothing to them, and they thought of it only as a rather dull story. The quickest way to a child's heart is through a smaller child or a helpless animal. Thus my saviour was Pidgy.

'Thereafter, my daily progress reports consisted of ten per cent sailing and ninety per cent pigeon. Things changed at once. Bated breath greeted the appearance of the *Guardian* on my desk each morning, and the day I forgot to bring it my apologies were howled down in a most disrespectful manner! The gradual progress of the crosses across the blackboard map went almost unnoticed. The news of Pidgy's sad end broke on a Saturday. By Monday morning, of course, several of the children knew. Those who had not heard were stunned. Our dinner numbers were very late going up that day, and nobody put much heart into their arithmetic. But that bird had done a good job for me. For the first time, I began to notice some sympathy for the lonely man. Now, he was well enough on his way for them to wonder about his chances of a record. The voyage now held interest for them in its own right, and gasps of delight or dismay, as appropriate, now greeted each daily cross. They laughed at the beer can exhaust pipe. They goggled at the whales. They cheered when he arrived. Up to this time, Francis Chichester and I had been doing all the work. I felt it was high time I gave them some. I had some unprecedented response from some members. One, after a sterling three-page effort, put: "The End. Too tud to carry on." I gave him a star.

'One, looking into the deepest recesses of her memory, recalled: "He was rather late for the starting line. Two Customs came to search because they thought he was a smuggler. He was thumbpin about up on deck." One almost forgot the bird. There was just an afterthought, underneath the picture. "He called his pigeon Piggy." '

The *Guardian* summed up in a leading article:

'Francis Chichester's passage from Plymouth to New York, alone in his 13-ton cutter *Gipsy Moth III*, in the record time of thirty-three and a half days, can fairly be acclaimed as one of the great achievements of the sea. As a feat of human endurance (and at the age of sixty-one) it is outstanding: different in degree, for such things are incomparable, but making the same kind of sustained demand on will-power as climbing a high mountain without oxygen. The gear of a 13-ton yacht, normally sailed by a crew of six, would tax the strength of most men to handle alone. Chichester has not only sailed his yacht single-handed across the Atlantic, but driven himself day and night to race her. And his race was, perhaps, the purest form of human competition in that he was racing solely against himself and his own record for the same crossing set up in 1960.

'He has failed in one sense—his personal ambition was to achieve the crossing in thirty days. But by any other standard his achievement will seem complete; and some measure of it may be gained by considering that his closest rival in the 1960 race, Colonel H. G. Hasler, took forty-eight and a half days to make the passage. Readers of the *Guardian* have been able to follow Chichester's voyage day by day by radiotelephone. The radiotelephone is not new, but its use in a small sailing boat to speak across ocean distances is unique. At the outset of *Gipsy Moth*'s voyage it was held that if messages were received from her half-way across the Atlantic it would be as much as could reasonably be hoped. About 40 degrees west of Greenwich was regarded as the probable limit of radiotelephony from a small battery-operated set. New York is 73 degrees 50 minutes of Greenwich, and Chichester was still talking to the *Guardian* off Long Island. This is an immense achievement for British radio engineering, and the credit goes fairly to Marconi Marine, the designers of *Gipsy*'s radio equipment, to the Exide batteries which powered it, and to the marine services of the Post Office, which maintained a constant watch for *Gipsy*'s calls and made communication with her, often in conditions of great difficulty.

'*Gipsy*'s telephone was used to report a yachtman's voyage, interesting and unusual, but in world terms scarcely of deep significance to humanity. The experience gained, however, is capable of being put to many uses, and the new range of radio-telephony that she has opened may serve to make life happier and safer for people in ways still unguessed. It has been a brave adventure by a brave man.'

At the Receiving End
BY DAVID FAIRHALL

___

IF you ever drive along London's North Circular Road, heading east past Hendon Stadium, you may just have noticed an anonymous brick building looking like something between a factory and an office block. There is no name outside, no imposing entrance, no distinctive feature but its drabness. Yet it is the centre of a world-wide network of radio communications operated by the GPO.

The concrete halls are packed with wire, plugs and dials. Apart from the control room that is, where the engineers on duty sit quietly talking, almost chatting with their opposite numbers at sea, in Africa or the Far East. This professional nonchalance is characteristic and deceptive. An antidote, perhaps, to the inevitable tedium of shiftwork, although a glance at the equipment that each has to maintain is enough to kill the idea of its being simply routine.

When we arrived to take our first calls from Francis Chichester, the staff's reception was understandably tentative. Some lunatic trying to drown himself in the Atlantic—expecting to maintain contact over 3,000 miles of ocean with no more than a 60-watt transmitter. There was the usual difficulty in explaining what a 13-ton ocean racing cutter actually amounts to, and the only other yachts on the list of registered call signs seemed to be the kind one associates with Mediterranean millionaires.

The strength of the story which grew from Chichester's daily call soon began to surprise the GPO staff as much as those who were reporting it. The Chief Engineer, Mr Gray, was enthusiastic from the start and a great deal of the trip's success as a journalistic exercise was due to the thorough organization provided by him and his assistants. The tape recording of each conversation, for example, proved immensely valuable. When Chichester had been roused by his alarm clock at, say, four a.m. to make his call, possibly after only a couple of hours' exhausted sleep, he was in no state to repeat himself two or three times because reception was poor. We rarely failed to sort out the details, however, after playing the critical phrase back a few times.

The first operators to call for *Gipsy Moth III* were polite and faintly amused, but they soon became as involved as we were. The technical situation made this inevitable, for even with three great aerials trained on *Gipsy Moth*'s estimated position from different parts of the country, it was often hard work finding her faint signals. Her transmitter was much less powerful than a normal ship's radio, even if the batteries had been fully charged. Once Chichester's voice came through, however faint, it was immediately recognizable through the racketing interference; a distinctive intonation as he called GCN 3, London, GCN 3, London. The booming whine of the searching receivers would quieten as they settled on the frequency and we switched to each in turn to see which had the best circuit.

Before long, engineers began dropping in to see how *Gipsy Moth* was getting along, or whether reception was really as good as they had heard. In fact, the quality was several times compared favourably with radiotelephone calls from a big passenger liner. The pigeon attracted a good deal of interest once it arrived, and when a technical crisis developed over charging the batteries advice on wiring and voltages was always available. By this time we had switched the calls from early morning to late at night to make them less of a strain for Chichester (reception was not good enough during the day) and each meeting seemed likely to be the last. When Chichester came to rewire his batteries for charging by the main engine, the engineers explained after his call that one wrong connection could flatten them in a few minutes. We waited anxiously until the next night when a calm, clear voice assured us that he was well aware of the danger and we need not have worried.

Over the month's voyage we built up a curious relationship with Chichester, the more so for my brother, who had previously met him for only a few minutes. One of us would sit in the dingy box of a studio, talking at a microphone and straining to catch the reply through headphones, while the other plotted positions on the chart or assembled a message. During the early part of the trip the calls were a downright nuisance for a man who had more than enough to keep his boat moving at full speed while eating, sleeping and navigating. But towards the end he confessed that he had come to appreciate his daily contact with normal existence.

At our end we tried, though pretty hopelessly, to visualize what was happening out there. Using a long distance telephone is always a feat of imagination; the fact of intervening space is as difficult to grasp as the speed of an aircraft from the passenger's seat. When the man on the other end is bracing himself against an Atlantic swell, with nothing but ocean for hundreds of miles around, it becomes an impossibility. The fascination comes in trying. Occasionally Chichester would try to convey things direct—'Can you hear those waves crashing on the deck?' Normally his habitual understatement prevailed—'You know it's quite rough out here'—but either way we knew that we could never really know.

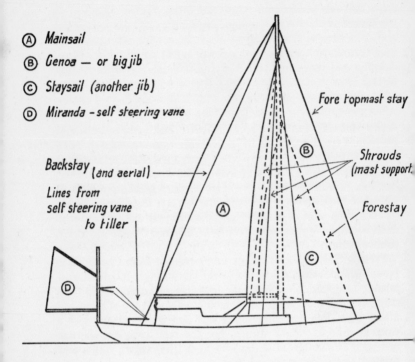

Ⓐ Mainsail
Ⓑ Genoa — or big jib
Ⓒ Staysail (another jib)
Ⓓ Miranda – self steering vane

Fore topmast stay

Backstay (and aerial)

Lines from self steering vane to tiller

Shrouds (mast support)

Forestay

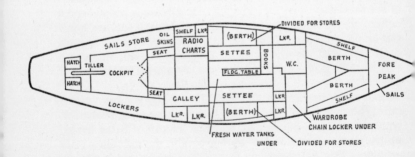

SAILS STORE

OIL SKINS

SHELF | LKR

RADIO CHARTS

DIVIDED FOR STORES

(BERTH) | LKR

SHELF

BERTH

SEAT

SETTEE

BOOKS

W.C.

HATCH

TILLER

COCKPIT

FLDG. TABLE

FORE PEAK

HATCH

SEAT

GALLEY

SETTEE

BERTH

SHELF

SAILS

LOCKERS

LKR. | LKR.

(BERTH)

LKR.

LKR.

WARDROBE
CHAIN LOCKER UNDER

FRESH WATER TANKS UNDER

DIVIDED FOR STORES

About Gipsy Moth III

Gipsy Moth III was designed by Robert Clark in 1957, and built by John Tyrrell at Arklow in Ireland. She was launched in 1959. She is 39 feet 7 inches long overall, with a waterline of 28 feet, a maximum beam of 10 feet 1¾ inches, and draws 6 feet 5 inches. She has an iron keel of 4½ tons. Her Thames Measurement is 13 tons, her gross tonnage 10¾ tons, and her net registered tonnage 9½ tons. She is built of mahogany planking on oak frames, with deck beams of spruce. Her deck is of half-inch plywood, with a rubber surface.

Francis Chichester sailed her single-handed from Plymouth to New York in 1960, to win the world's first single-handed transatlantic race, and to establish the first acknowledged record for a single-handed crossing from Plymouth to New York of forty and a half days. For that voyage she was rigged as a sloop, with a wooden mast of hollow spruce. For the 1962 crossing, she was re-rigged as a cutter, to designs by John Illingworth, with a new mast of metal alloy by Sparlight.

The plan above (not drawn to scale) gives a simple explanation of her masthead cutter rig. The difference between a sloop and a cutter is that a sloop has only two sails, a mainsail and one headsail or jib, whereas a cutter has stays for setting two headsails before the mast, commonly called a jib and staysail, although a very large jib is also often called a 'genoa'—a term which Francis uses in his narrative to describe his big jibs.

Both as a sloop and as a cutter, *Gipsy Moth III* has what is called 'Bermudan rig'. This means that her mainsail is triangular, without an upper spar or gaff, and that instead of being hauled up the mast on rings, it goes up a groove in the mast on a track or slides. The Bermudan rig is aerodynamically more efficient than the older gaff rig for small sailing boats, because the mainsail is tight against the mast, and there is no gap through which wind power can be lost. A disadvantage of the rig is that to get the necessary sail area from a triangular sail the mast has to be a good deal taller than the mast of a gaff rigged vessel of similar size: *Gipsy*'s mast is 50 feet high. Modern methods of staying masts and of mast construction, enabling them to be made much lighter than they used to be, have largely overcome the disadvantage of tall masts.

The areas of *Gipsy Moth*'s suit of sails are: mainsail, 276 square feet; genoa, 420 square feet; No. 2 jib, 250 square feet; No. 3 jib, 134 square feet; spitfire or storm jib, 65 square feet. Her trysail, another storm sail which can be set in place of the mainsail, has an area of 144 square feet. Her sails are all of Terylene.

The movement of a sailing boat through the water is complex, because at any given moment it is subject to a number of air and water forces, some of which may be in opposition to one another. There are three main points of sailing: running with the wind aft—that is, coming from the stern; reaching, with the wind coming from the side or quarter; and beating, with the wind coming from ahead. In running, the boat is simply blown forward, the only resistance being the friction of the hull in moving through the water. In reaching, the boat is blown both sideways and forwards; the keel resists sideways movement, and the rudder maintains forward motion in the desired direction. Some wind force is naturally lost because of that element in the wind which is trying to blow the boat sideways. In beating, the boat is sailing *against* the wind; the sails are sheeted in hard, and the wind, in flowing over them, leaves a momentary vacuum at the leading edge of the sails into which the boat is sucked. This explains the ability of a sailing vessel to move forwards against the wind. At the same time, of course, the wind is trying to drive her backwards, and as the boat heads nearer into the wind a point is reached at which the power of the wind flowing over the sails is not sufficient to overcome the direct force of the wind blowing against her. No sailing boat can sail dead into the wind. The angle of nearness to the wind at which she can still make forward progress is determined by her rig, and sailing qualities, and by the skill of her helmsman. The angle that a boat sailing against

the wind makes with the direction of the wind is called her degree
of 'pointing'. Where, in his narrative, Francis Chichester records
that *Gipsy Moth* was 'pointing rather too high', it means that the
boat was beginning to sail rather too close to the wind for
maximum efficiency.

Wind forces are commonly measured on the Beaufort Scale,
called after Admiral Beaufort who devised it. The forces in the
Beaufort Scale, with the wind speed in knots, are:

Force	Wind speed in knots
0	Under 1
1	1 – 3
2	4 – 6
3	7 – 10
4	11 – 16
5	17 – 21
6	22 – 27
7	28 – 33
8	34 – 40
9	41 – 47
10	48 – 56
11	57 – 65
12	Above 65

At Force 8 the wind officially becomes a 'gale'. Anything over
Force 8 is a violent wind, and Force 12 is the official beginning
of a hurricane. In great storms wind speeds may be well over
100 knots.

A knot is a speed, not a distance. One knot is one nautical mile
per hour. A nautical mile is rather longer than a land or statute
mile, being 6,080 feet, or 1·1515 land miles. Six knots is roughly
7 m.p.h.

GEORGE ALLEN & UNWIN LTD

London: 40 Museum Street, W.C.1

Auckland: 24 Wyndham Street
Bombay: 15 Graham Road, Ballard Estate, Bombay 1
Buenos Aires: Escritorio 454-459, Florida 165
Calcutta: 17 Chittaranjan Avenue, Calcutta 13
Cape Town: 109 Long Street
Hong Kong: F1/12 Mirador Mansions, Kowloon
Ibadan: P.O. Box 62
Karachi: Karachi Chambers, McLeod Road
Madras: Mohan Mansions, 38c Mount Road, Madras 6
Mexico: Villalongin 32-10, Piso, Mexico 5, D.F.
Nairobi: P.O. Box 12446
New Delhi: 13-14 Asaf Ali Road, New Delhi 1
Sao Paulo: Avenida 9 De Julho 1138-Ap. 51
Singapore: 36c Prinsep Street, Singapore 7
Sydney, N.S.W.: Bradbury House, 55 York Street
Toronto: 91 Wellington Street West